WHO I AM ?

Selamat pagi travelers! (hello in Indonesian) let me introduce myself, I am Lilian, a second-year French business student, during my studies I had the chance to live in Bali for 5 months mainly in Uluwatu near Bingin Beach but I was able to visit the whole island including the Gili Islands. I was able to meet many Balinese people and even become friends with some. I had the chance to discover this island from a different angle, while living there I had an unusual experience. After 5 months, I acquired a lot of skills and advice and I wanted you to share my experience through this guide!

WHY THIS GUIDE?

The "Essentials in Bali" travel guide is based on an observation that I was able to observe through meeting other tourists, friends and family who came to Bali. Many told me that they were not well informed about the island and its culture, and sometimes had a rather false image of the island which is the symbol of overtourism. Indeed, Bali does not stop at this image! This guide is designed to give you a complete Bali travel experience beyond the tourist trails. I favored practice over theory in writing this guide.

As was the case for me before my departure, I bought a lot of guides and read a lot of books. Looking back, I realized that some of them were missing a lot of the island or important information, including local addresses, which is unfortunate. So that's why I decided to write and share my experience, bringing you advice and my points of view as well as contacts from local friends!

But it doesn't matter your level of travel experience or your specific expectations. If you are a family or a group of friends, I have made sure that the content is broad enough to suit all desires and expectations.

By browsing its pages, you will find practical information, advice and personalized recommendations that would have been very useful to me before leaving, the emblematic places, and the unique experiences that Bali has to offer. **The goal ?** May this guide help you step by step in planning and carrying out a tailor-made trip, adapted to what you want.

All photos in this guide were 95% taken with my phone! I own all the rights to it.

SUMMARY

Introduction — 5
- Bali in 3 words! — 6
- Why choose Bali for your vacation? — 7
- Who is this guide for? — 8

1. Prepare for your trip to Bali — 10
   - When to go to Bali? — 11
   - How to get to Bali? — 12-13
   - Administrative formalities and visas — 14-15-16-17
   - Health and safety: practical advice — 18-19-20
   - Budget and currency — 21-22

2. Discover Bali: the essentials
   - The most beautiful beaches in Bali — 24
   - Top 5 emblematic temples to visit — 25-26-27
   - The rice terraces of Bali — 28
   - Activities: hiking, surfing, diving. — 29-30-31
   - Local markets and crafts — 32

3. Explore the different regions of Bali — 34-35-36
   - Ubud: cultural and artistic center of Bali — 37-38
   - Restaurant and accommodation ideas — 39-40
     - The surroundings of Ubud — 41-42-43
     - Uluwatu: heavenly beaches and surf spots
   - Restaurant and accommodation ideas — 44-45
     - The Gili Islands: excursions from Bali — 46-47-48
   - Restaurant and accommodation ideas — 49-50
     - Canggu: the city of expatriates — 51-52-53
   - Restaurant and accommodation ideas — 54-55
     - Seminyak: Where you never sleep — 56-57-58
   - Restaurant and accommodation ideas — 59-60
     - Amed: between sea and mountains — 61-62-63
   - Restaurant and accommodation ideas — 64-65

- - Sanur: la moderne — 66-67-68
- Restaurant and accommodation ideas — 69-70
  - Sidemen: nature waiting for you — 71-72-73
- Restaurant and accommodation ideas — 74-75
  - Nusa penida: the magnificent one! — 76-77-78
- Restaurant and accommodation ideas — 79-80
  - Nusa Lembogan: the discreet one! — 81-82-83
- Restaurant and accommodation ideas — 84-85

4. Living in Bali: accommodation, food and transport
  - The different types of accommodation in Bali: hotels, villas, guesthouses. — 87
  - Where to eat in Bali: specialties and restaurants — 88
  - Getting around Bali — 89

5. Practical advice and tips
  - Communication and internet in Bali — 91
  - A bit of Bahasa — 92
  - Respect for Balinese customs and traditions — 93
  - Avoid common tourist traps and scams — 94

- **Bonus**
  - \+ An ideal course in 2 weeks — 95 to 98
  - \+ 100 places and addresses in Bali — 99 to 112

INTRODUCTION

"To travel is to give meaning to life, to discover new horizons, and to be enriched with each step"

Bali is more than that! And yes, how many times have I heard this phrase from other travelers who had experienced the adventure. Let's go back to basics, Bali is an Indonesian island located in the Sunda archipelago, between the islands of Java and Lombok. Known as "the island of the gods" or "the island of a thousand temples", Bali has been a popular tourist destination for around 8 years; its popularity has exploded!

Here is a general presentation of Bali:
Incredible landscapes: Bali is characterized by a diversity of landscapes, ranging from heavenly beaches to mountains like Mount Batur and rice fields. Volcanoes, including Mount Agung. And honestly, we never get tired of it!

A Rich Culture: Balinese culture is impressive! Full of ancestral traditions. Sacred temples, such as Besakih Temple and Uluwatu Temple, occupy the landscape, but also many others, while religious ceremonies are visible in the streets every day, colorful offerings at the entrances of houses including your guesthouses and hotels are an integral part of daily life.

Art and Craft: Bali is famous for its traditional crafts, including wood carving, painting, jewelry making, and fabric making. Local markets are full of artisanal treasures that showcase the know-how and creativity of Balinese artisans.

Gastronomy: Balinese cuisine offers exotic flavors and delicious dishes. From traditional Indonesian dishes such as nasi goreng (fried rice) and mie goreng (fried noodles) to Balinese delicacies such as babi guling (roasted suckling pig), not to mention the fruits that grow on the island, one cannot forget is always very surprised.

Activities: Bali offers a multitude of activities for all tastes and budgets. From water sports like surfing, diving and snorkeling to rice field hikes, yoga, spas and the vibrant nightlife of Canggu, there is always something to do in Bali.

In summary, Bali is much more than just a trendy vacation destination on social media. It is a true paradise that seduces travelers with its landscapes, its culture and its gentle way of life. Once you taste it, you never want to leave. Bali offers an unforgettable travel experience

BALi iN 3 WORDS...

BALi
Province of Indonesia | Capital Denpasar

RESiDENTS
The Balinese

FLiGHT
18h flight | London-Denpasar (Time varies depending on the stopover)

PASSPORT
Valid for 6 months after return date + visa required (see page 15)

CASH
Indonesian rupee | IDR, rupiah
1£ = 20 920Rp

JET LAG
+7 in summer (+8h in winter)
7 hours in London = 15 hours in Bali

SURFACE
5 600Km2

POPULATiON
4.3 million inhabitants (2023)

RELiGiON
90% of Balinese are of Hindu faith

WHY CHOOSE BALI FOR YOUR VACATION?

Bali in 2023 will have more than 5.2 million tourists, but why?

For your vacation, the question of where to go inevitably arises at some point. Bali offers a unique blend of beauty, ever-present culture and diversity of activities that make it a top destination for travelers from around the world.

First of all, Bali attracts tourists with its natural beauty which is simply breathtaking, like a dream. From white sand beaches to transparent waters, whether in Uluwatu or the Gili, there is something to be surprised about! But also the rice terraces and volcanoes, the island offers breathtaking landscapes, the landscapes are just incredible!

Then, Balinese culture is rich and fascinating. It is part of the cultures in the world still existing. From sacred temples with offerings and traditional dances, to local crafts and cuisine, Bali offers an authentic immersion in a culture very different from ours. Despite mass tourism, its traditions have not been disrupted.

In addition, the activities offered in Bali are as numerous as they are exciting. Whether you are a fan of water sports (surfing, jet skiing), outdoor hiking, yoga or wellness, or looking for relaxing moments discovering nature, Bali has something to offer everyone . This is why I love this place so much!

Finally, the hospitality and smiling welcome of the Balinese make each visit a human experience. Having lived with them, they are very generous and helpful, but know how to respect their cultures and traditions! And you will be welcomed with kindness and generosity. I will have thousands of anecdotes to tell you, **believe me!**

In summary, choosing Bali for your vacation means choosing adventure, discovering a culture and relaxation. It's choosing a destination that will remain engraved in my memory, even after 5 months of having lived there I still think of the island every day.

Dreamland beach

Monkey forest

WHO IS THIS GUIDE FOR?

This guide is for anyone planning to explore Bali, whether they are travelers or first-timers who know nothing about it.

Whether you are solo looking for new experiences, a couple, a family who wants to relax or a group of friends who want to party, this guide will provide you with valuable information for planning a stay in Bali and especially getting out of the beaten paths and avoid tourist traps!

No matter your age, interests or budget, in this guide you will find practical advice, activity recommendations and tips to fully enjoy everything there is in Bali.

Whether you want to relax on the Gili beaches, explore the temples in the south of the island, venture into the rice fields of Sidemen or Ubud or simply discover Balinese culture, this guide will accompany you at every stage of your trip, helping you helping to create memories on this pretty special island.

At the end of the guide you will find a bonus including a list of more than 100 addresses and places, as well as an ideal itinerary for two weeks!

When we go on a trip or settle abroad, we all have this question in mind: **how to organize our trip so that it goes as we hope?** Choosing this guide is already the assurance that you know and have a good basis in mind so that everything runs smoothly...

9 KEY STEPS...

1— Choose the dates and length of stay: determine when you want to leave based on your vacation and how long you want to stay in Bali. In my opinion, the minimum is 10 days. Consider the seasons and climate.

2- Check your passport and check visas: make sure your passport is valid for at least six months after your planned arrival date. Also check visa deadlines for nationals of your country.

3- Book your flights: search and book flights to Bali. Compare prices and routes to find the best option for your budget and preferences. Attention ! Some layovers may be long and require a change.

4— Look for accommodation: Compare the different accommodation options in Bali, from villas to hostels to hotels. Book in advance to get the best rates and ensure you have a place. For my part, I have always booked on Booking and it has always worked.

5- Plan your activities: make a list of places you want to visit and activities you want to do in Bali. This may include cultural tours, excursions, surfing sessions, jungle treks, etc.

6- Learn about the local culture: respect local rules and adopt appropriate behavior.

7- Plan your budget: establish a budget for your trip, in fact, Bali may seem inexpensive when taking into account expenses such as flights, accommodation, food, activities and souvenirs.

8- Make sure you have travel insurance: take out travel insurance that covers medical expenses, trip cancellation and lost luggage.

9- Pack your bags: prepare a list of everything you will need, taking into account Bali's climate (e.g. mosquito repellents) and the activities you plan to do. Don't forget essential items such as medicines, travel documents. The sockets remain the same as in France.

HAVE A GOOD TRIP !

WHEN TO GO TO BALI?

CLIMATE

There is a hot and humid climate with two main seasons: the dry season between April and September and the rainy season between October and March. The rainy season alternates between rain and good weather. The center of the island is very humid, especially between December and early March.

TEMPERATURES

The average temperature in Bali is 26°C. In the mountains, it can be cooler, especially in the evening, at night and at dawn, as at Mount Batur.

IDEAL SEASON

For various reasons, the best time to come to Bali is from April to June and September, just before and just after the peak tourist season. It is still the dry period and the weather is less humid.

ANECDOTE

Personally, I went from September to January and I was quite worried about the weather. For me, September-October remains the ideal time to come to Bali and enjoy good weather with fewer tourists. It is true that from November it can rain, but the weather remains very pleasant! The center of the island is much more exposed to rain than the far south, I was in Uluwatu and most of the time it rained very rarely!

PS: Don't be afraid of those who will say to you: "Are you going to Bali in December? It will rain !» If you stay there at least two weeks and get moving, you will see good weather!

HOW TO GET TO BALI?

BY PLANE :

- Bali has one main international airport, Ngurah Rai International Airport, also known as Denpasar Airport (IATA code: DPS). It is the main entry point for travelers to Bali.

- Book a flight: Search for flights to Denpasar Airport from your departure location. Many international airlines serve this airport, including Emirates, Garuda Indonesia, Singapore Airlines, AirAsia, Qatar Airways and KLM, offering a wide range of options when it comes to prices and routes.

- Make sure your passport is valid for at least six months beyond your planned arrival date in Bali. If necessary, organize your other travel documents such as plane tickets, hotel reservations and insurance.

- Flight to Bali: Once on board your flight, enjoy the journey to Bali. The duration of international flights to Denpasar Airport may vary depending on the departure point. Direct flights from Asia generally last between 3 and 6 hours, while those from Europe or America can extend to 10 to 20 hours or more, with one or more stopovers. Stopovers are often planned in Dubai, Doha, Amsterdam, Madrid, Bangkok, Taipei, Singapore, Istanbul, Hong Kong, Jakarta, etc.

- Arrival in Bali : Upon arrival at Ngurah Rai International Airport in Denpasar, go through immigration formalities, collect your luggage and follow the signs to exit the airport.

Attention ! When you leave the airport, around ten drivers will be waiting to take you. Don't do it ! Because the price is really too expensive, around 450,000 rupiahs, while **Gojek or Grab** only costs 350,000 rupiahs to get from the airport to Ubud, for example. Plus, you don't have to worry about unpleasant surprises! Indeed, I notice that many people worry about transfers from the airport to their destinations.

I wanted to talk to you about Gojek and Grab which are taxi service applications which are similar to other taxi or VTC booking applications like Uber. I invite you to download them to your smartphones, create an account, then book a trip with a driver in a few clicks.

PRICE OF PLANE TICKETS:

The prices of plane tickets to go for example from London to Bali can fluctuate depending on different factors, such as the **booking period** (the high season corresponds to the months of July and August, as well as the end-of-year holidays), the airline or even flight availability. Here is a general estimate of the prices you can expect :

- Prices for flights from London to Bali typically range from around £264 to £738, depending on the time of booking, the airline, and the specific dates of travel

- During the peak tourist season in Bali, such as during the summer holidays or the Christmas and New Year period, airfare prices tend to be higher. Direct flights from London to Bali are rare and often more expensive. Most flights include one or more stopovers, typically in hubs like Singapore, Doha, or Kuala Lumpur

- Airlines offering flights with a stopover can sometimes offer cheaper prices than direct flights. However, this may extend the duration of the trip. Personally, I took tickets in August for September, Allez Paris - Singapore-Bali and on the return Bali-Dubai-Paris. Price: 1400€/1175£

- It is recommended to research several flight comparison sites and book in advance to find the best deals. The following sites: Opodo, Kayak, Google flights, Skyscanner. It is advisable to book on **Tuesday and Thursday** to benefit from the most advantageous prices!

Tirta Empul

ADMINISTRATIVE FORMALITIES AND VISAS

The paperwork and **visa requirements** for traveling to Bali depend on your nationality and the length of your stay.

- Visa exemption for many countries: Nationals of many countries can enter Indonesia, including Bali, without a visa for short-term tourist stays. This visa exemption is generally valid for a period **of up to 30 days**, but this may vary by country. Be sure to check the latest information on your country's Indonesian embassy or consulate website.

- Visa on arrival **(VOA)**: valid for Australian, American and Uk citizens. If you are a national of a country that is not visa-exempt or plan to stay longer than the permitted visa-free period, you can obtain a visa on arrival at Denpasar (Bali) Airport or at other points of entry into Indonesia. This visa on arrival is valid for a period of 30 days and can be extended once for an additional period of 30 days.

- Visa before arrival: If you plan to stay more than 30 days in Indonesia or are not eligible for a visa on arrival, you may need to obtain a visa before arrival. There are different types of visas, including tourist visas, business visas and long-stay visas. Procedures and requirements vary depending on the **type** of visa and the country of issue and the price too. It is recommended to contact the Indonesian embassy or consulate in your country for accurate visa information.

- Traveling with a minor: for a minor to be able to leave the territory and travel to Indonesia, they must be accompanied by at least one of their parents. The latter must then present:
- A passport valid for the entire duration of the stay (at least 6 months after the date of entry into the country);
- A document proving that he is indeed the father or mother of the child and that he has parental authority (civil status certificates, family record book).
- Visas are also required for children!

Pay attention to the validity of the passport! **Make sure your passport is valid for at least six month**s beyond your planned departure date from Indonesia. The Indonesian authorities are very careful.

It is important to check the latest visa information and requirements before traveling to Bali, this may change at the last minute. Entry requirements may also vary depending on the current political and health situation. While speaking with Balinese people, I realized that during the Covid crisis everything had been turned upside down. In the event of an exceptional situation, take your precautions!

VISA ON ARRIVAL (VOA) AND E-VISA ON ARRIVAL (E-VOA)
30 DAY SIGHTSEEING TRIP

DURATION:
The visa on arrival and the e-visa on arrival allow you to stay 30 days in Indonesia. These are single entry visas, you are only allowed to enter the country once.

CONDITIONS
- Have a passport valid for at least 6 months
- Show a return ticket

PRICE
Visa on arrival and e-visa on arrival cost 500,000 IDR (25£).

HOW TO GET IT?

ON LOCATION You can obtain a visa directly upon your arrival in Indonesia. Ask for it at the counter located just before immigration when you arrive.

ELECTRONIC VERSION (E-VOA)

In 2022, Indonesia launched a new electronic visa on arrival system. First called e-VOA (Electronic Visa On Arrival). You can apply for and pay for your visa online before departure. Website: https://molina. migrasi/. Beware of scams and malicious sites!

It is advisable to apply for your e-VOA between 48 hours and 14 days before your arrival in Indonesia.

The elements necessary to prepare the e-VOA request are:
- **Passport valid for at least 6 months**
- **Digital photography**
- **Continuation ticket**
- **E-mail address**
- **Credit card**

Once the application is completed and the payment validated, you can directly download your visa. You also receive it by email. From the issuance of your e-VOA, you have 90 days to enter Indonesia.

This system speeds up the procedures upon your arrival, you only have to present your visa confirmation to the immigration agent. Having experienced it, it is not uncommon for there to be a lot of people at the airport and for it to take between 1 hour and 3 hours to get out.

"LOVE BALI" TOURIST TAX

Since February 2024, you must pay a tourist tax called "Love Bali" in addition to your visa if you visit this island. It costs 150,000Rp/7£. It is recommended to pay online before your departure. You can pay by credit card on the application or on the "love Bali" website. You will receive proof of payment called a "Levy Voucher" by email.
If you have not paid the tax online, you can pay it at the counter available at the Bali airport and port. This tax aims to protect culture and provide institutions with the means to finance infrastructure on the island. The tax must have been paid before you leave Indonesian territory.

PROLONGATION

The visa on arrival and the e-visa on arrival are renewable once. It is therefore possible to stay up to 60 days in Indonesia with these visas.
You must make the request no later than three working days before the end of your visa.

VISA EXTENSION (VOA) ON-SITE

You must go to one of the immigration offices, there are everywhere, especially in Denpasar for those who are in Uluwatu. It's in Jimbaran. You will need to fill out a form, give your passport and your return ticket proving your exit from the country.
You will have to come back three days later to pay 500,000 IDR (25£). You will be made to wait and called to have your photo and fingerprints taken.
You will have to come back a third time to collect your passport with the visa extension directly on the passport.

EXTENSION OF THE E-VOA ONLINE

Since January 2023, thanks to the new e-VOA, it is possible to do this process online and pay for the renewal directly.
It costs the same price = 500,000 IDR/25£.
As soon as your e VOA is registered by the immigration officer at customs, you can request an extension. Simply log in to the same site where you created your e-visa and extend it. This is the government portal.

EXCEEDING

Since 2019, if you overstay your visa you will have to pay a fine of 1 million rupiahs (47£) per day for the first 60 days of overstay.
After these 60 days, you risk being blacklisted from the country. There is no exception, you will not be able to board until you have paid the fine. Pay attention and respect deadlines!

In case of doubt, questions or to obtain information, do not hesitate to contact the institutions in your country. Here are their contact details:

EMBASSIES AND CONSULATES

EMBASSY OF THE REPUBLIC OF INDONESIA IN CANBERRA, AUSTRALIA
Address: 8 Darwin Avenue, Yarralumla Canberra, ACT 2600 Australia
+61262508600
canberra.kbri@kemlu.go.id
+61262733545, +61262736017

CONSULATE GENERAL OF THE REPUBLIC OF INDONESIA
Address: 236-238 Maroubra Road, Maroubra, New South Wales (NSW) 2035
(02) 9314 0872
IMIGRASI : imigrasi.sydney@kemlu.go.id ,
KONSULER : consular.sydney@kemlu.go.id,
LAINNYA : info.sydney@kemlu.go.id
+61 2 9349 6854

CANADA EMBASSY OF INDONESIA IN OTTAWA
Address: 55 Parkdale Avenue, Ottawa, Ontario K1Y-1E5 Telephone: +1 613 724 1100 Visit website Opening hours: Monday to Friday 9 a.m. to 5 p.m.

EMBASSY OF THE REPUBLIC OF INDONESIA IN WASHINGTON D.C. THE UNITED STATES OF AMERICA
+1 (202) 775 5200
washington.kbri@kemlu.go.id
+1 (202) 775 5236

The Consulate General of the Republic of Indonesia in New York
Address: 5 East 68th Street New York, NY 10065
Phone: (212) 879 - 0600
Fax : (212) 570 - 6206
Website: kemlu.go.id/newyork

The Consulate General of the Republic of Indonesia in Los Angeles
Address: 3457 Wilshire Boulevard Los Angeles, CA 90010
Phone: (213) 383 - 5126
Website: kemlu.go.id/losangeles

EMBASSY OF THE REPUBLIC OF INDONESIA TO THE UNITED KINGDOM, IRELAND, AND IMO in LONDON
Address: London 30 Great Peter Street, London SW1P 2BU, United Kingdom
(+44-20) 7290-9600
contact@indonesianembassy.org.uk
(+44-20) 7491-4993

HEALTH AND SECURITY :

- Check recommended vaccinations: Before you leave, consult a healthcare professional to make sure your vaccinations are up to date and ask if there are any recommended vaccinations for your trip to Bali. This may include vaccines for hepatitis A and B, typhoid, rabies and other diseases.

- There are pharmacies **(Apotek)** everywhere. Be careful though, because, as you are tourists, people can try to sell you anything and everything!

- Protect yourself from mosquitoes: Bali is an area where mosquito-borne diseases, such as dengue fever, circulate, but there are no cases of malaria on the island. **But be careful** on Lombok! It is important to take precautions to avoid mosquito bites. Use mosquito repellent, wear long, light clothing, and use mosquito nets if necessary. **Anecdote:** I was stung more than 60 times!

- If necessary, there is a list of doctors and hospitals on the French Embassy website.

- Drink bottled water: **never drink tap water**. To avoid water-related illnesses, such as the famous "Bali Belly", make sure to drink bottled or filtered water. Avoid ice cubes in drinks and raw foods washed down with tap water. Buy bottled water even to rinse your teeth and if you buy food be careful when you wash them!

- Adapt to the climate: Bali's climate is tropical, with hot and humid temperatures all year round. Dress lightly and wear sunscreen with a high SPF to protect against UV rays. I myself have caught several **sunburns** even when the weather is bad, because the UV rays remain! Also make sure to stay hydrated by drinking plenty of water regularly.

La favela

- In small warungs, be careful with undercooked foods and especially fruits and vegetables, as hygiene may leave something to be desired. **Anecdote :** Be careful of spicy food, especially "sambel", a typical very spicy sauce that made me sick for three days!

- Avoid risky excursions : When taking part in activities like diving, surfing or hiking, make sure you choose reputable operators. Follow the safety instructions and do not take unnecessary risks. Some people regularly have accidents, especially on the islands of Nusa Penida and Gili. Be careful, because they don't always provide life jackets! There can also be **big waves** when you go diving, especially towards Nusa Penida to see the manta rays.

- In the ocean: All the beaches are affected by very strong waves and surprising currents, I myself fell into the water several times, particularly on Uluwatu, known for surfing.

- Be Vigilant Against Crime : Although Bali is generally considered a safe destination for tourists, it is important to remain vigilant about carjacking and tourist scams. Be careful, for example, of Instagrammers on scooters: they may snatch their phones. **Anecdote :** the Balinese leave their helmets on their scooters, because no one steals them. Indeed, in religion, if someone steals, they will be prosecuted sooner or later!

- In terms of drugs: Indonesia is formally positioned to fight drug trafficking, **THERE IS ZERO TOLERANCE even for foreigners and tourists**. Exemplary behavior is expected, because consumption is subject to serious penalties, and trafficking is punishable by the **death penalty!**

- Respect the local culture: learn about Balinese traditions and respect them during your stay. For example, on **Nyepi Day,** it is important to respect the rules and not leave the house. Dress appropriately when visiting temples or religious sites. Women who are having their periods should not enter certain sacred buildings. Be respectful to local residents. Ask locals if you take photos of them!

- **MONKEYS :** the island in places is heavily populated by monkeys, particularly in the Monkey Forest, Ubud, the Uluwatu temple and its surroundings. You should not wear sunglasses, jewelry or shiny objects, as this will attract their attention! If he climbs on top of you to attack you, stay still!

- **False guides :** during your visits, particularly to Mount Batur and around the Uluwatu temple, people will try to approach you. Do not follow them: they are false guides who will charge you to "protect yourself from monkeys". Systematically refuse!

Nyang-Nyang Beach

HEALTH AND SAFETY: PRACTICAL ADVICE

Before you leave, here are some tips not to forget!

- Plan for **travel assistance** (assistance, repatriation). Like europ-assistance, chapka, amex....Certain bank card **contracts** such as gold cards already include this.

- **Find out more** on the website of foreign affairs of your country in case there are any last minute changes.

- Consult your doctor in advance before departure

- Prepare a first aid kit : usual medications and prescriptions; Above all, take medication for stomach aches, as well as creams (sunscreen, insect bites). **Tip :** if you have a very bad stomach and you don't have any medicine, go to **Apotek** and ask for **Norit**, the Indonesians use it for stomach aches.

EMERGENCY NUMBER

112, 110 Police
113 Firefighters
114, Ambulance
115, Rescue

BUDGET AND CURRENCY

To plan your budget and manage your money during a trip to Bali, here is some information on the currency and costs of your stay :

- **Currency :** The official currency of Indonesia, including Bali, is the Indonesian Rupiah (IDR). Banknotes are available in denominations of 1000, 2000, 5000, 10,000, 20,000, 50,000 and 100,000 rupees. The coins are available in denominations of 100, 200, 500 and 1000 rupees. Attention ! Always convert your money with your phone to double check prices. We tend to underestimate the value.

- Exchange Rate: The exchange rate of the Indonesian Rupiah against other currencies may vary. It is recommended to check current exchange rates before your departure and monitor fluctuations during your stay. It is sometimes interesting to change your currency at a certain period.

Attention ! You should always check during a transaction whether the office is reliable. The conversion rate must be displayed in front of you and the person at the exchange office must count the notes and make the transaction in front of you. You will also need to sign a document attesting to the exchange.

- **The cost of living in Bali** being very low, one might think that it is not necessary to plan a large budget. Indeed, everything is cheaper than here, but in tourist areas the prices are higher like Kuta, Seminyak, Ubud and especially Canggu, while the more remote areas can be more affordable everything will depend on your level of requirements in terms of accommodation, catering and activity. Some beach clubs, restaurants and hotels can be as expensive as ours sometimes. If you want to have an affordable stay, you will need to not stay exclusively in tourist areas.

- Accommodation : Accommodation prices in Bali vary depending on the type of accommodation, location and facilities. You can find options ranging from cheap hostels for 6£ per night to luxury hotels and villas for several hundred euros per night – there are plenty to choose from!

- Food : Meals in Bali can be very affordable, especially if you eat at warungs (small local restaurants), but also warung makan (street stalls). **Anecdote :** I already paid 0,5£ for a meal! Prices vary depending on the type of cuisine if you eat European style it will be more expensive. In more local areas, prices will obviously be lower.

SOME EXAMPLES :

1 month at the gym in Uluwatu "Muscle beach club": 850,000 Rp, or 40£.
Rental of a scooter for one month: Rp 750,000, or 35£.
1 litre d'essence : 8000 Rp/0,38£
1 night at a hotel on Nusa Penida (breakfast included): Rp 258,000/12£ per person per night.
Chicken Fried Rice/Riz frit au poulet au local stall : 40 000 Rp/1,88£ Entrée au temple d'uluwatu : 50 000Rp/ 2,3£
1 hour of body massage at the U.Spa: 140,000 Rp / 6,6£ Climb of Mount Batur with a guide via GetYourGuide (breakfast included): 724,000 Rp, or 33£.
Gojek scooter ride from Uluwatu to Seminyiak: Rp 76,000, or 3,6£.

PAYMENT METHOD :

- Apple Pay is accepted in many places, Visa and Mastercard bank cards are **VERY PRESENT.**

- Inform your bank that you are going on a trip to avoid unpleasant surprises, blockages and hidden fees. Also, for money withdrawals. Indeed, in Bali, cash is everything: in some places, you can only pay in cash! In particular to pay for entrances to certain beaches.

- There are a lot of bank ATMs, **BUT** some are defective, look at the reviews on Google first and be careful. Some swallow the cards and don't give you your money back!

- **PRECAUTION on the islands:** there are a lot of power cuts. Several of my friends had their cards swallowed and were unable to get them back. **My tip :** Exchange money in Bali before your trip to the islands so you don't have to worry about your bank cards.

- Depending on the bank, there is a commission that applies to fees ranging from 3 to 5% per withdrawal. In addition, it is rather rare to be able to withdraw more than 1,500,000 IDR in one go.

TIPS

WISE: Wise is an app that makes international money transfers easy by offering favorable exchange rates and transparent fees. Users can send money in different currencies across the world.

2.Discover Bali: The Essentials

Gili Trawangan

THE MOST BEAUTIFUL BEACHES IN BALI

Although Bali is not known for its beaches! There are some beaches in the south of the island and on the islands that are worth a visit! Please note that some beaches charge a fee.

📍 Nusa Lembongan

📍 Uluwatu Beach   📍 Gili Trawangan   📍 Diamond beach

📍 Kuta Beach

TOP 5 EMBLEMATIC TEMPLES TO VISIT

The temples in Bali are like the Eiffel Tower in Paris: it's unmissable! There are them all over the place, so I recommend you visit at least two. They are important symbols of Balinese culture.

📍 TIRTA EMPUL TEMPLE

Tirta Empul Temple is a sacred place where people purify themselves in holy water springs.

📍 BESAKIH TEMPLE

Besakih Sanctuary is the most important temple complex on the island, located on the slopes of the sacred Agung volcano.

📍 ULUN DANU BRATAN TEMPLE

Perched on the banks of Lake Bratan, it offers a very beautiful landscape

📍 TEMPLE LOT LAND

The Tanah Lot temple is the iconic temple! It extends into the ocean off the coast of Bali, providing a spectacular setting for religious ceremonies and sunsets.

25

⛯ TEMPLE D'ULUWATU

Uluwatu Temple, perched on a cliff overlooking the Indian Ocean, offers breathtaking views and is home to monkeys. There is also the famous Kecak dance show.

SOME ADVICE WITHIN THE TEMPLES

Visiting Balinese temples is a fascinating experience that allows you to discover the culture and spiritual side of Bali. Here are some tips to make the most of this experience:

- **Firstly,** temples in Bali often require payment, their prices are between 25,000Rp and 75,000Rp per person, they are used to finance and conserve Balinese heritage. There is **often** a rate reserved for tourists. You can often only pay in cash.

- Respect **the clothing rules :** temples are sacred places where it is important to show respect. Dress properly by wearing covering clothing, avoid shorts, tank tops and clothing that is too short. There are sarongs available which are often necessary to cover the legs; they can be borrowed at the entrance to the temple.

- Take off your shoes: In most Balinese temples, it is customary to remove your shoes before entering. **Do the same thing!**

- Be respectful: Maintain a respectful and quiet behavior inside the temple. Avoid speaking loudly, laughing loudly, running, or disrupting any religious ceremonies that may be taking place. **That would be very frowned upon!**

- Pay attention to the indications: respect the indications and the rules specific to each temple. Some temples may have special rules to follow, such as not climbing sacred structures or not taking photos in certain areas. Above all, don't step on the offerings!

- Avoid touching the statues and **offerings! :** In many temples, it is considered impolite to touch sacred statues or offerings left by worshippers.

THE RiCE TERRACES OF BALi

Welcome to Bali, the island of rice terraces which, among the most beautiful rice fields in Bali, has three rice terraces that stand out for their beauty. I had the chance to visit 2 out of the 3 and I assure you that in real life they are as magnificent as in the photos! The rice fields are located in the center of the island between Ubud and Sidemen which are the wettest corners of the island. Be careful, there can be a lot of mosquitoes around.

Start your journey at Jatiluwih, a UNESCO World Heritage Site, where rice terraces spread out, creating an entire landscape. The rice fields here are very large and this creates large valleys that extend to the mountains behind.

Continue your way towards the **rice fields of Tegallalang**, knowing that you will have to pay to access them. These rice fields are very popular due to their proximity to the famous Beach Club Cretya, known for its impressive cascading rice terraces. The ingenuity of Balinese farmers is reflected in the arrangement of the fields. There are plenty of activities in the valley to do, like the famous swings.

Finally, don't miss the rice **terraces of Sidemen :** they are, in my opinion, the most beautiful and are located at the foot of Mount Agung. The atmosphere here is incredibly calm and authentic. You can see the traditional and authentic Bali before your eyes. You can see local farmers working there. Walk the trails through the rice fields, the picture is magnificent!

List of rice fields to see:

- Tegalalang Rice Terraces
- Jatiluwih Rice Terraces
- Sidemen Rice Terraces
- Pupuan Rice Terraces
- Rendang Rice Terraces

ACTIVITIES: HIKING, SURFING, DIVING, ETC.

Lovina

DIVING AND SNORKELING

Diving in Bali is an incredible experience, I guarantee it! It's not expensive and it's beautiful. You will also have the opportunity to go see the **dolphins** in Lovina, all to the north of the island. And also the corals around the coast are crazy!

The waters of Bali offer a wide variety of dive sites; They are found everywhere, but particularly in the north and northeast of the island, and they are suitable for all levels, from beginners to experienced divers. **For example in Amed,** the spectacle of wrecks and corals is not to be missed. You can also explore the waters of Nusa Penida, where there are manta rays further offshore.

For a truly unique experience, head to Tulamben and see the famous Liberty Shipwreck, a wreck covered in colorful corals. I had the opportunity to dive in Lovina, Nusa Penida, Nusa Lembongan and Amed. Each time it was different, but incredible! I rented a GoPro, which allowed me to take lots of photos to preserve these memories.

Diving costs between **9£ and 29£,** some hotels offer excursions directly. Note on Gili Trawangan many people offer you a global pack of around 250,000Rp for 2 and they take you diving to see the famous underwater statues and they drop you off on Gili Meno which is a magnificent island! Don't hesitate to go around the island and they will pick you up to return to Gili Trawangan.

HIKES

Hiking in Bali allows you to discover different landscapes: from rice terraces to cliffs, there are lots of things to see while walking, and it is really very beautiful, like in Jatiluwih. For those who want to see the most beautiful sunrise, climbing Mount Batur is an iconic experience. The sunrise is the reward after 2 hours of walking through the mountain. And believe me, it's very physical, but it's worth it!

Those who love adventures can climb to Mount Agung the highest point on the island, the highest peak in Bali, at the top, the panoramic views of the island and beyond reward the effort, while the Besakih temple, located at its feet, adds another dimension to the hike.

Finally, for those who prefer tranquility, there are several waterfalls to see near Munduk. It's the authentic side of the place and it's very relaxing. Attention ! It is much colder there than on the rest of the island; there are also forest walks to do. What's great about these corners of the island is that you really get to know what Balinese culture is, because you leave your hotel and you can see the way of life of the locals live in front of you!

SPA AND MASSAGE

Bali spas are renowned for their traditional Balinese massage techniques, and yes! there are massage parlors everywhere and when you know that 1 hour of massage costs around 5£, this is one of the essential things to do! Massages in Bali are renowned because they use specific techniques that combine gentle movements with moderate pressure to relax the muscles. For a more luxurious experience, the seaside resorts of Nusa Dua and Seminyak offer very renowned spas with personalized services and specific treatments, particularly very present in the hotels which are very established in these areas.

SURF

Bali offers a surfing experience for all levels, from beginners to professionals. International surfing competitions have been held on the island for over 30 years, many surfers from all over the world come to Bali for surfing. Surfing is an iconic activity on the island, so if you have the time, I highly recommend you try it!

Be careful, Bali is famous for its surfing competitions because in places the currents and waves can be very strong!

Where to surf?

For beginners :
Kuta beach is perfect for learning to surf with its calm waves and sandy bottom unlike other coasts. Many surf schools offer lessons for all ages. There is also Canggu, with its varied beaches and bohemian atmosphere, is popular with surfers. The Batu Bolong and Echo Beach spots offer waves for all levels.

For the experienced :
Uluwatu, on the Bukit Peninsula, is a must-visit destination for experienced surfers. The hilltop bars and restaurants offer stunning views of the surfers. Bingin Beach is ideal for those seeking tranquility, Bingin is popular with intermediate and advanced surfers. Because the waves are blocked on part of the coast, this allows you to train well!

Some practical advice...

Rent your equipment from local surf shops and follow the instructors' advice. Respect safety rules and pay attention to sea conditions.

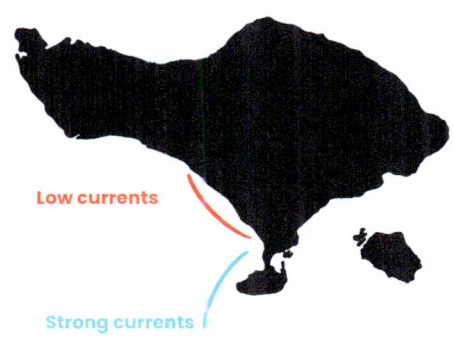

Low currents

Strong currents

31

LOCAL MARKETS AND CRAFTS

Denpasar local market

Bali has great local crafts and yes! **Living there,** I quickly realized that there were many markets, food and non-food, as well as several artisan shops.

Ubud, Capital of Crafts : Ubud, which is known for its rice fields, is also home to a vibrant craft market. There are many craftsmen everywhere, especially those who work with wood. The Ubud market is a must. It is located near the Monkey Forest for craft lovers: it's great! ! Take a stroll through its aisles, I'm sure you'll find what you're looking for.

In Kedonganan, the traditional fish market transforms into a spectacle of floating markets at sunrise. Here, fishermen sell their daily catch directly from their boats.

The Sukawati Art Market : Sukawati, located not far from Ubud, is known for its art market, the Pasar Seni Sukawati. This market is great for those looking for unique souvenirs like colorful sarongs, wooden sculptures, traditional batiks and decorative items that are much cheaper than back home. It's great for those who want to shop and what's more, **you can negotiate directly** with the manufacturer.

In Bali, some tourists forget that they are in Indonesia and that there is an incredible culture to discover, whether it is coffee, wood, weaving and even jewelry! There are several markets that display local crafts in Canggu, Uluwatu or Seminyak. Remember to bargain respectfully and immerse yourself in the unique experience of shopping the Balinese way.

3. EXPLORE THE DIFFERENT REGIONS OF BALI

Nusa Lembongan

UBUD AND ITS SURROUNDINGS: CULTURAL AND ARTISTIC CENTER OF BALI

DISTANCE FROM UBUD :

Uluwatu- Ubud: 3 hours (depending on traffic) 55 km distance
Seminyak- Ubud: 2 hours (song traffic) 50 km distance
Kuta-Ubud: 2h30 (depending on traffic) 60 km away

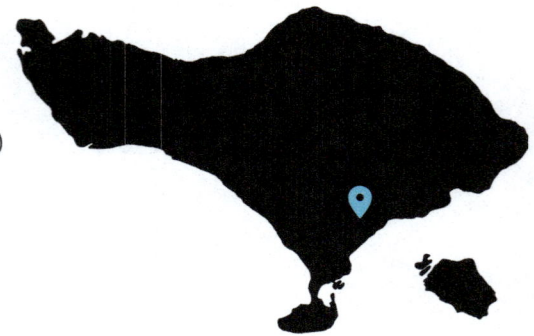

WHY VISIT UBUD ?

Ubud is often considered an important stopover during a stay in Bali, located in the heart of the island. It is an unmissable destination for its authenticity; you will see, it is quite different from the rest of the island. Then, the setting is surrounded by rice fields and jungles, Ubud offers spectacular views, including the Tegallalang and Jatiluwih rice fields. The cool thing about Ubud is relaxing and yes! it's full of spas, yoga centers and meditation retreats, perfect for recharging your batteries.

SOME ADVICE AND INFORMATION :

Transport :
Ubud is approximately 1.5 hours' drive from Ngurah Rai International Airport. Here are some options for getting around:
- **Be careful,** traffic is huge on the main streets, especially around Jl. Raya Ubud, Jl. Hanoman and Jl. Monkey Forest. The side streets are quieter.
- Taxi and Private Driver: Book a taxi or private driver for a direct and comfortable ride from the airport. **Tip :** Try to ride a Gojek or rent a scooter to go faster!
- **Anecdote :** my family spends more than 6 hours to go from Uluwatu to Ubud because of traffic jams, so traffic is no joke, especially in high season.

Accommodation:
- **Tip :** I suggest you stay outside the city center to be quiet, about 20 minutes walk from the city center. I advise you to book in advance, especially during the high season between April and September when prices can very easily increase!

Budget :
- Ubud offers dining, shopping and accommodation options to suit all budgets, from warungs to gourmet restaurants. But overall, prices will be rather high for Bali, because it is a very touristy area.

THE ESSENTIALS

MONKEY FOREST

Open every day from 9 a.m. to 6 p.m. The Monkey Forest is a sacred forest in the heart of the city. There is a long walk to take, traditional shows to see and ancient temples and above all many monkeys. The monkey is venerated in the Hindu religion, through the god Hanuman, the site is sacred and protected. The monkeys roam freely next to you. **Be careful,** do not carry shiny and valuable objects! No sunglasses either. Monkeys can pounce on you; if so, stay up and wait for them to come back down! **Price: 100,000Rp**

CASCADES TIBUMANA

Open every day from 8 c.m. to 5 p.m.
The Tibumana Waterfalls near Ubud are one of Bali's best-kept secrets. It's hidden in the middle of nowhere in impressive vegetation. Accessing Tibumana is an adventure, with a path crossing the forest and green rice fields. The waterfall flows into a natural pool, perfect for a dip. The waterfalls are less crowded. Price: 15,000Rp

TEGALLALANG RICE FIELDS

Open every day from 8 a.m. to 5 p.m., The Tegallalang rice fields, located a few kilometers from Ubud, are an incredible landscape. This iconic landscape of Bali is perfect for walks, these rice fields are known to be very Instagrammable with the famous swings. The surrounding cafes allow you to enjoy the view while having a Balinese coffee. Price: 15,000Rp

◉ CRETYA UBUD

Open every day from 8 a.m. to 5 p.m., Cretya is the Beach club in Ubud, there are lots of swimming pools, a restaurant, and lots of activities downstairs including super beautiful rice fields to discover. I advise you to come before 3 p.m. in high season, **entry costs 100,000Rp per person**. Please note, for families, please note that swimming pools are prohibited for children under 18 years old.

AT THE HEART OF CULTURE

CASCADE SUMPAMPAN

Open every day from 8 a.m. to 5 p.m.
The Sumpampan waterfall, located near Gianyar, is a pearl of Bali. Accessible by a path which is itself an adventure! Be careful of the very steep stairs, Sumpampan is ideal for visitors who want to see natural sites. The waterfall flows into a natural pool where you can swim and enjoy the water. Less crowded than other sites, Sumpampan promises an authentic experience, great for those who want to be in the middle of nature. Price: 10,000Rp

UBUD PALACE

Open every day from 8 a.m. to 7 p.m.
Ubud Palace, or Puri Saren Agung, is a must-see in Bali. Located in the heart of Ubud, this palace is typical of Balinese architecture and culture. It is still the residence of the royal family of Ubud.
You can visit the gardens, including the courtyard which is decorated with sculptures. In the evening, there are traditional Balinese dance performances. Entrance is free, but shows cost around IDR 100,000 per person.

MUSEUM PURI LUKISAN

Open every day from 9 a.m. to 5 p.m.
It is the oldest art museum in Bali. It features an extensive collection of traditional Balinese art, from paintings to sculptures, exploring the artistic evolution of the island.
The decor of the museum is very nice, surrounded by a garden. Entrance costs approximately IDR 85,000 per person, including a welcome drink.

CASCADES TEGENUNGAN

Open every day from 8:30 a.m. to 6 p.m.
Located 10 kilometers south of Ubud, it is one of the most impressive waterfalls in Bali. It is surrounded by vegetation, to access it, you go down a staircase lined with local shops. Below, the view of water flowing down into a natural pool is spectacular. Visitors can swim or rest on the surrounding rocks. Tegenungan is an **ideal half-day trip.** The place is fully equipped: there are showers and changing rooms. Price: 20,000Rp

HOUSING IDEAS

HOTEL MENZEL UBUD

Menzel Ubud is a hotel in the heart of the rice fields of Ubud, ideal for a weekend. The rooms and villas, decorated in a traditional Balinese style, offer breathtaking views of the gardens or rice fields. The hotel offers different services. In particular, you can have breakfast by the pool, which is incredible! In addition, the hotel offers Balinese massages, treatments, and yoga. The restaurant serves local and international cuisine which is very good. **I recommend it. I stayed there!**
Price: From 57£/night

AGUNG RAKA RESORT AND VILLAS

Located in the rice fields of Ubud, accommodation varies from rooms to private pool villas, all with stunning views of the rice fields. An infinity pool and a restaurant serving traditional cuisine. Agung Raka Resort and Villas' prime location allows easy access to Ubud's main attractions, such as the Monkey Forest and local markets. Price: from 20£/night

CAPELLA

It is a luxury hotel nestled in the jungle of Ubud, designed by the famous architect Bill Bensley. This hotel stands out for the decor around it and these tents, decorated in a colonial style with Balinese touches, including private pools and panoramic jungle views. Facilities include an infinity pool, spa, and several gourmet dining options. Conveniently located, Capella Ubud allows you to explore Ubud's rice terraces, temples, and local markets. If you want to treat yourself as a couple, this is the ideal address! Price: 553£/night

BARS AND RESTAURANTS

AMBER UBUD BAR

Open every day from 2 p.m. to 11 p.m.
The bar offers cocktails in a beautiful setting with a panoramic view of the Balinese jungle. Be careful, the price is quite high. Price: from 200,000Rp.

RESTAURANT MOXA

Open every day from 10 a.m. to 9 p.m.
The restaurant is located in the middle of greenery, the concept is healthy and Vegan cuisine, it's worth the detour! Price from 80,000Rp.

TAMAN DEDARI RESTAURANT

Open every day from 10 a.m. to 11 p.m.
This restaurant is well known for its decor, the menu is Western. Price from 70,000Rp.

RESTAURANT ZEST

Open every day from 8 a.m. to 10 p.m.
Zest, in Ubud, offers vegan cuisine in a chic and green setting. The restaurant is out of the ordinary! Price from 100,000Rp.

FORT AT MANDAPA

Open every day from 6 p.m. to 11 p.m.
It offers a culinary experience in private bamboo huts on the banks of the Ayung River. The setting is incredible! Price from 200,000Rp.

WAYAN CAFE

Open every day from 8 a.m. to 11 p.m.
In the heart of the Balinese world, local specialties guaranteed. Lots of gardens, buffet at 200,000Rp

CAFÉ POMEGRATE

Open every day 9 a.m.-9 p.m. 360° view of the rice fields. Ideal at sunset. The cuisine is Western, the choice is vast! The pizza is 65,000Rp.

Taman Dedari

THE SURROUNDINGS OF UBUD

THE ASCENT OF MOUNT BATUR

Located at 1,717 m above sea level, it is the second largest volcano in Bali. The ascent starts from the Toya Bungkah car park. Experience: I have done Mount Batur myself, and I will give you some advice. Bring good shoes and warm clothes, as it is cold at night when you go up. **Indeed,** the ascent is done at night around 4 a.m. and yes you have to be motivated! Generally on organized tours you are provided with sticks and a flashlight.

At the summit, you are usually given breakfast and tea. The reward is the view of the valley and the lake, it's sublime. However, climbing Mount Batur is not a walk in the park! I personally do sports and I can assure you that I had difficulty climbing it, the crossing is long and the paths are very steep, it slips hence the importance of having good shoes and it can happen whether the weather is rainy. You have to be hooked, because in total, with the climb and descent, more than 4 hours of **hiking await you!**

Let's review the essential points...

Duration of the climb: 2 hours
Contact : Whatsapp +62-812-3966-4605
Start of the trek: 40 km northwest of Ubud, 1 hour drive. Departure is at 4 a.m.
- You can organize yourself in different ways such as through your hotel, specialized agencies or directly with the Batur guides association on site.
- Please note: this climb is only done with local guides, do not venture alone

Personally, I booked on the Get your guide website. The price starts from 37£ and includes transport to Uluwatu.
You have 2 options
- 1) Leave Ubud at night to go on the excursion
- 2) book a night directly at the foot of the volcano.
- Avoid the rainy season (Dec-Apr.): because the climb is not great! I myself fell while climbing, because the terrain was slippery and the view can be very foggy.

LES ALENTOURS D'UBUD, MUNDUK

Many people leaving Ubud choose to go see Munduk and its surroundings, particularly to see nature, the viewpoints, the waterfalls and the small village of Munduk. Many paths leave the village towards waterfalls, rice fields and plantations... In short, Munduk is perfect for hiking!

CASCADE DE MUNDUK

Open every day 9 a.m. - 5 p.m. It can be accessed by following the signs from the road. There is a path that goes along the river and takes you to several waterfalls: Labuhan Kebo, then Melanting. Price: 20,000Rp

ARIS HOMESTAY

This is a guest house, with a magnificent view overlooking the valley and mountains. The 360-degree view of the landscape is definitely worth the detour, Price: 12£/night

WARUNG CLASSIC

Open every day 11 a.m.-10 p.m. The view is very nice. I recommend going there at the end of the day when the sun sets to enjoy the panorama. Price: from 80,000Rp

Some info...

- 1.5 hour journey from Ubud
- No gojek or grab take a driver or rent a scooter
- 800 m d'altitude
- A cooler climate, counting 20°C.
- The climate can be humid
- **Advice: 1 day visit maximum, the village is small**
- Bring warmer clothes
- No ATM in the village.

ULUWATU : HEAVENLY BEACHES AND SURF SPOTS

DISTANCE FROM ULUWATU :
- Uluwatu- Ubud: 3 hours (depending on traffic) 53 km distance
- Uluwatu- Canggu : 1h30 (selon le trafic) 34 km away
- Uluwatu- Kuta : 1h (depending on traffic) 23 km away

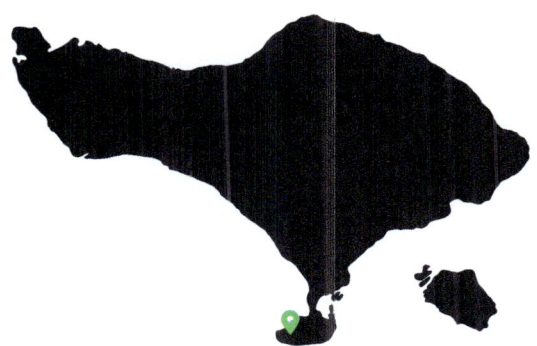

WHY VISIT ULUWATU ?

Uluwatu is known as Bali's surfing village; it is currently expanding. In fact, expatriates have recently started to take an interest in it. This is why Uluwatu is often overlooked by guides to Bali, which revolts me, because Uluwatu is essential for me! Visiting Uluwatu means discovering very nice landscapes, the most beautiful beaches on the island, surf spots. Whether you're a surfer or not, it's beautiful. The little plus is that Uluwatu is much quieter in terms of traffic than Canggu, Seminyiak or Kuta. Then, in Uluwatu there are many very famous beach clubs!

SOME ADVICE AND INFORMATION :

- **Climate :** It benefits from better weather. **Anecdote:** my friends said it rained in Canggu, but not in Uluwatu. As the latter is more exposed to the winds, it benefits from better weather.

- **Beaches :** The southwest coast of the peninsula is home to beautiful sandy beaches. Be careful, most are accessible by steep stairs. There is always a charge for parking and most entrances as well. Swimming is possible, most often at high tide. Popular beaches include Padang Padang, Bingin, and Nyang Nyang. Surfers of all skill levels can enjoy the waves, but some beaches are more suited to experienced surfers.

- **Budget :** Uluwatu is often less expensive than Canggu or Ubud because it is still under development and you will find plenty of projects from real estate developers.

- **Tip :** rent a scooter to visit Uluwatu, it's very practical and you'll save a lot of time!

THE ESSENTIALS

SINGLE FIN

Open every day from 8 a.m. to 10 p.m., and until 1 a.m. on Sundays.

This emblematic bar and restaurant is perched on the cliff, it is one of the best-known beach clubs in Bali. The ocean view is incredible. **Why go there?** It's the perfect place for sunsets. Sundays are particularly popular; there is often live music and a big atmosphere. If you have the chance, go for it! Price: 30,000Rp for a bintang beer, it's Indonesian beer.

PLACE DE PADANG PADANG

It is accessible by small stairs, this beach is famous for the turquoise water which is also visible from the road just above. This beach is very famous and it's great, it's a famous surf spot. Price: 10,000Rp

ULUWATU PURA LUHUR TEMPLE

Open every day from 7 to 7 p.m. For dance shows, there are two: one at 6 p.m. and the other at 7 p.m. Situated on top of a cliff at 70 meters, Pura Luhur Uluwatu Temple is one of the most important and iconic temples in Bali. It is also very **important** for the Balinese! Why go there? In addition to its religious significance, the temple offers views of the ocean, especially at sunset. For taking photos, it's great! Kecak dance shows are a well-known activity there, but planned in advance. Price: 50,000Rp

⦿ ULU CLIFFHOUSE

Open every day from 8 a.m. to 11 p.m. This is the **Uluwatu beach club** perched on the cliffs, offering spectacular views of the ocean. The design is very modern: there is an infinity pool, beds, a restaurant and access to the beach. The restaurant offers a wide menu. In the evenings, Ulu Cliffhouse hosts exclusive DJs and events, providing a perfect festive atmosphere to enjoy the evenings. I find that it is clean, modern and that the staff is always on top. And, for once in Bali, I find that this "beach club" is suitable for families! Price: from 150,000Rp

BEACHES AND SUNSETS

BALANGAN BEACH

Balangan beach is quite special: it is long and its sand is white. As for surfing, if you don't practice, you'll come here more to watch the surfers. Price: 10,000Rp

MELASTI BEACH

It is accessible by small stairs, this beach is famous for the turquoise water which is also visible from the road just above. This beach is very famous and it's great, it's a famous surf spot. Price: 10,000Rp

NYANG-NYANG BEACH

It is less known and less crowded, Nyang Nyang is an isolated beach which offers a quiet setting, much less touristy than the others! Ideal for those looking to get away from the crowds, this beach offers miles of sand. Price: 10,000Rp

RITUAL

Open every day from 2 p.m. to 10 p.m. The Ritual Bali is located near Sunset Point and perched on the cliffs, offering breathtaking views of the Indian Ocean especially at sunset. This beach club has a restaurant, a swimming pool, sometimes gives yoga classes and sometimes organizes rather nice events. The shape of the building, which resembles a sail, is quite unusual. Price: Coke at 35,000Rp

DREAMLAND BEACH

A beautiful beach with perfect waves for surfing and an ideal setting for relaxing. At Dreamland, the waves are calmer than at other beaches ideal for surfers. **Tip :** Grab a coconut from the bar and watch the sunset. Free admission

IMPOSSIBLE BEACH

It is a very discreet wild beach, only accessible at low tide. It is famous among surfers and it is near Padang Padang. It's a great place to admire the sunsets, but you have **to be careful of the stairs!** Free admission

HOUSING IDEAS

SIX SENSES ULUWATU

Located on a cliff with a view of the ocean, Six Senses Uluwatu is a luxury hotel, if you want to treat yourself this is the ideal place! The hotel offers villas, a spa, several dining options and wellness activities, honestly the location of the hotel is just amazing. Price from 503£/night

ASHANA HOTEL

The rooms are well appointed with air conditioning, TV and free Wi-Fi. The hotel has an outdoor swimming pool in the heart of the resort, a restaurant offering local and international cuisine, a 24-hour front desk and travel desks. **Personally** having stayed there the staff is great, the Ashana Hotel is perfect for exploring Uluwatu. The little extra: you can do a lot of things on foot, starting from the hotel, directly on the main beaches and their many beach clubs and restaurants. Price: from 26£/night

Apurva Kempinski Bali

APURVA KEMPINSKI NUSA DUA

Apurva Kempinski Bali, opened in 2019, is located on the coast of Nusa Dua, offering stunning views of the Indian Ocean. Inspired by Balinese and Javanese traditions, this establishment is the equivalent of a palace. It's just huge! For me, **it is the most beautiful hotel in Bali!** It offers suites, private villas with swimming pools, several gourmet restaurants, a world-renowned spa. **Tip :** No need to spend thousands of dollars to have this experience. Instead, opt for dinner at the beach restaurant, which is more affordable. Price from 258£/night

BARS AND RESTAURANTS

MORABITTO BINGIN BEACH

Open every day from 2 p.m. to 10 p.m. The Morabito Art Cliff in Bingin is a bar with a breathtaking view of the ocean, it is an unmissable place for sunsets. Part of a complex featuring luxurious villas and installations by French designer Pascal Morabito. **Fun Fact**: You'll often hear French music.

WAROENG DE DUSUN

Open every day from 11 a.m. to 10 p.m. Guaranteed local meal. This was my favorite restaurant in Uluwatu. It offers all Indonesian specialties, such as nasi goreng or ayam satay (peanut chicken). Few tourists venture there, but honestly, it's worth the detour!
Anecdote: we paid 13£ to eat for 6!

LOCAL STALL

Open every day 8 a.m. to 10 p.m. The local warung is a small, typical Indonesian restaurant where you can taste local dishes at very affordable prices. Menus vary, but generally include specialties such as nasi goreng, satay, and mie goreng. This one has been modernized. **Tip:** opt for the nasi goreng ayam. Price: from 1,6£

TABU

Open every day from 5 p.m. to 11 p.m. Tabu Restaurant is a chic and contemporary place. The restaurant stands out for its atmosphere with the famous symbol of the restaurant on fire, which fuses Japanese and Mexican specialties. Tabu is the ideal place for an evening, there is often house music and DJs after 10 p.m., with friends it's great! Price: from 150,000Rp

DAPUR BALANGAN

Open every day 12 p.m. to 8 p.m. Guaranteed local meal! The food is typical, but very good; we compose our own dish. This restaurant is a small, inexpensive shop, prices starting from 30,000Rp.
Anecdote: the boss is Indonesian he always wears a hat and is very welcoming

45

THE GiLi ISLANDS : EXCURSiONS FROM BALi

DiSTANCE FROM THE GiLi ISLANDS :

- Departure by boat from PadangBai port towards the Gili Islands. The crossing lasts 2 hours 40 minutes.
- Ubud — Padang Bai Port: approximately 50 minutes (depending on traffic); distance: 37 km.

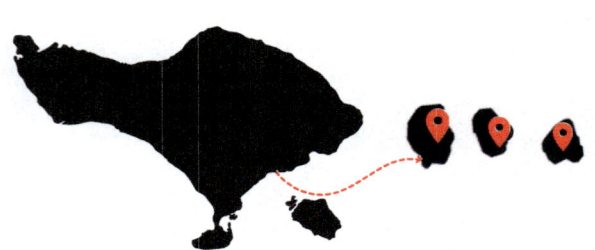

WHY VISIT THE GiLi ISLANDS ?

The Gili Islands, located off the northwest coast of Lombok in Indonesia, are a trio of small islands, including Gili Trawangan, Gili Meno, Gili Air. Firstly, like Bali, the Gili Islands are known as a paradise of sandy beaches and turquoise waters. **The little extra :** the Gili Islands are free of cars and motorbikes; travel is done on foot, by bicycle or horse-drawn carriage.

SOME ADVICE AND INFORMATION :

Culture :
- The Gili and Lombok islands are Muslim, like Bali, which has an official Hindu religion. You often hear prayer especially on Gili Trawangan.

Access and Transportation:
- How to get there ? The Gili Islands (Gili Trawangan, Gili Meno, and Gili Air) are accessible by boat from Bali and Lombok. Fast ferries depart daily from Padang Bai and Serangan ports in Bali. The journey takes approximately 1.5 to 2 hours from Bali and 15 to 30 minutes from Lombok. Entrance to the islands is chargeable, you will pay at the port of arrival (compulsory passage). **Contact for the boat: Whatsapp** +62-812-3890-2120

Practical advice:
- Payment methods: It is advisable to withdraw sufficient money before arriving. Anecdote: there are a lot of power cuts on the islands, your card can get stuck in the ATMs.

Health and security :
There are no hospitals on the islands, but medical clinics are available for basic care. For serious medical emergencies, it may be necessary to travel to Lombok or Bali. The islands are generally safe, but it is always advisable to exercise caution. The Gili Islands are poorer than Bali.
Attention ! On Gili Trawangan, we can offer you hallucinogenic mushrooms during the evenings. **Don't take them!** And watch over yourself.

THE ESSENTIALS

DIVING EXCURSION AND VISIT TO GILI MENO

Gili Meno has one of the most beautiful beaches and the best preserved coral in the archipelago. **Please note:** Gili Meno is very wild. Almost nothing has been built there, which is what makes it magnificent. Here, the stars are the turtles. Threatened with extinction, they are very fragile. Follow a few rules: don't touch them, don't try to follow them and don't feed them. Opposite the Diana Cafe, dive 100 m from the shore with a mask and snorkel to see the Nest, 48 statues sculpted in a semi-circle created by artist Jason de Caires Taylor. Very often, you are offered a pack of 250,000Rp per person from Gili Trawangan including diving and the excursion to Gili Meno You can go around the island on foot in 1 hour! **Tip**: always negotiated!

VISIT GILI TRAWANGAN BY BIKE

It is the largest and liveliest of the islands, known for its parties, bars and beach parties. Don't hesitate to go around the island by bike to admire the beaches and the turquoise water. The journey takes approximately 1 hour; halfway, don't hesitate to stop and have a drink on the beach, you will feel like you are alone in the world! Don't miss the night market either to taste local dishes, but be careful, as hygiene can leave something to be desired!
Price: around 2,5£ per day for renting a bike.

Gili Trawangan

BEACHES AND REST

GO KAYAKING IN GILI AIR

Explore the waters of Gili Air by paddleboard or, even better, by glass-bottom kayak, to see the many fish and, with a little luck, turtles! The water is just incredible and seminar in the Maldives! Price from 100,000Rp/h.

RELAX AND ENJOY

Quite simply, relax and this is surely the stage of your stay where you can just rest, sunbathe and walk around. The ideal length of stay on the Gili Islands is around 3 days. For beaches, choose those to the north or south, because the others are lined with hotels and therefore tourists. Most are lined with bars and restaurants. Watch the sunset from the west coast. Many swings are installed on the beaches all around the island. The little extra is free!

DIVING SPORTS

- Trawangan Dive resort, a very professional center, offers initiations to diving in swimming pools directly in those of the diving hotel from 600,000Rp

Leave directly from the beach with your mask and snorkel. To do at high tide! Watch out for the currents! To see more beautiful corals, embark on a day or half-day excursion to the different islands. Departure around 9-10 a.m. There are many guides who stand directly on the beach, near the landing stage, as well as in front of the snorkeling sites: Rental of masks and snorkels, approximately... 50,000Rp/day.

HOUSING IDEAS

MAHAMAYA GILI MENO

- Localisation: Gili Meno

This beach resort offers modern rooms. It's the ideal place for people looking for serenity! The beach is right next to the hotel, it's a dream! Services: restaurant on the beach, boat trips, diving. **The little extra** is that you are alone in the world around the hotel. Prices from 91£ per night.

TRAWANGAN DIVE RESORT

- Localisation: Gili Trawangan

The resort offers various rooms, it is very renowned for its diving facilities, the resort's diving center offers courses for all levels. Meals can be enjoyed overlooking the beach and ocean, while the bar is perfect for sunset cocktails as it is located directly on the beach. I stayed there and I can tell you that it is ideally located only a few minutes walk from the lively center of Gili Trawangan and the port, the resort allows you to enjoy the nightlife, shops and restaurants of the island while offering calm. Prices from 41£ per night.

UNZIPP BUNGALOWS GILI AIR

- Localisation: Gili Air

This establishment offers an authentic experience with its traditional wooden bungalows, surrounded by gardens. You can enjoy the outdoor swimming pool, relax in the common areas. The ideal location allows easy access to the beach, where you can swim, snorkel or simply soak up the sun. Price from 36£ per night

Trawangan dive resort

BARS AND RESTAURANTS

PACHAMAMA ORGANIC CAFÉ & RESTAURANT (Gili Air)

Open every day from 8 a.m. to 10 p.m. Bobo setting, stone floors, rope pendant lights. It's not by the sea, but the restaurant is worth the detour. As for the cuisine, it is inventive and careful. The cuisine is healthy and organic. It's well presented and the desserts are refined. Price from 80,000Rp

SCALLYWAGS BEACH CLUB (Gili Air)

Open every day from 7 a.m. to 10:30 p.m.
This beachfront restaurant offers international cuisine and fresh grilled seafood. Specialties: Seafood barbecue, steaks, fresh salads. The relaxing atmosphere with spectacular views of the ocean, ideal for a romantic dinner at sunset. Price from 100,000Rp

LA CALA (Gili Trawangan)

Open daily from 8:30 a.m. to 11 p.m. This restaurant specializes in Mediterranean cuisine, with tasty dishes prepared using fresh, local ingredients. The menu offers grilled meat skewers with salads and authentic tapas. La Cala offers a chic and relaxed atmosphere with trendy decoration. Guests can dine indoors or al fresco on the beach. The atmosphere is great! Price from 70,000Rp

TIKI GROVE (Gili Trawangan)

Open daily from 3 p.m. to 10:30 p.m. It is a charming restaurant and bar with a relaxed atmosphere and colorful Polynesian-inspired decorations. The bar serves cocktails, perfect for relaxing after a day of sightseeing. The friendly atmosphere and warm service make it an ideal place for an evening out. Tacos from 65,000Rp

DIANA CAFE (Gili Meno)

Open every day from 8 a.m. to 10 p.m., Very beautiful spot for the sunset. Very kind and welcoming staff. The choice of dishes is varied, the tempeh curry is to die for. And it's not expensive. I highly recommend ! Price from 40,000RP

MAHAMAYA (Gili Meno)

Open every day from 7 a.m. to 10 p.m. Waterfront restaurant, very varied menu, the only restaurant on the island that allows you to eat well apart from local dishes! Go there without asking any questions, the desserts are delicious. Price from 100,000Rp

CANGGU : THE CITY OF EXPATRIATES

DISTANCE FROM CANGGU :
- Canggu- Ubud: 1 hour depending on traffic, distance of 28 km
- Canggu- Sanur: 40 min depending on traffic, distance 20 km
- Canggu- Uluwatu: 1h20 depending on traffic, distance of 35 km

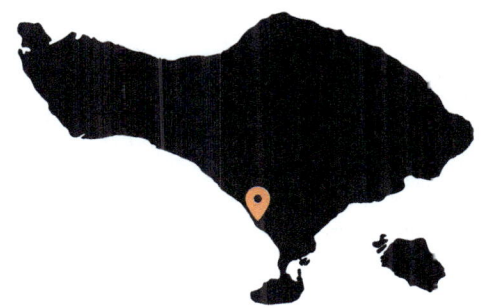

WHY VISIT CANGGU ?
In my opinion, Canggu is a city that must be visited for several reasons and in particular for its life which is quite unique on the island. But also its proximity to the Tanah Lot temple. Canggu is a great stop for those feeling homesick. There are indeed a lot of expatriates there as well as all the very westernized services that go with them! But Canggu is above all beaches where you can surf, places to go out, there are plenty of beach clubs! For those who want to go out, but also go to the beach, this is the ideal place.

SOME ADVICE AND INFORMATION :
Traffic :
Canggu is the tourist center of the island; traffic is therefore very busy there. So be careful when renting a scooter, because **there are a lot of accidents.**
- Scooter: Renting a scooter is the most convenient way to get around Canggu. Make sure you have an international driving license and wear a helmet. Contact **in Canggu WA**: +62-816-4743-261
- Taxis: For longer trips or in the evening, use taxis or ride-hailing services like GoJek or Grab.

Restore :
- Restaurants: Canggu has a lot of top addresses, but consider the fact that the prices are the highest on the island, because it is where the expatriates live.
- Bars and clubs: For nightlife, Canggu is great. There are a lot of beach clubs

Accommodation:
- Villas and Hotels: Canggu offers a very wide range of accommodation, Book in advance, especially in high season.

Security :
- Keep an eye on your personal belongings, especially in beach clubs and when riding a scooter, especially in busy areas.

THE ESSENTIALS

TEMPLE TANAH LOT

Open every day from 8 a.m. to 7 p.m. Located near Canggu, the Tanah Lot temple is one of the most emblematic religious sites in Bali. This temple is very beautiful: it is perched on a rock and it is an ideal place to admire the sunsets. And to discover Balinese culture.
Price: 60,000Rp for adults

GO SURFING AT ECHO BEACH

Echo Beach is one of the most famous beaches in Canggu; it is famous for its waves and its surfing atmosphere. This is a perfect beach for experienced surfers, but tourists can also enjoy the many seaside cafes. There are quite a few beach stalls with plenty of specialties. They serve grilled corn, but also barbecued seafood. There are surf sessions with equipment rental from 16£ per person.

GO TO LOVE ANCHOR

Open every day from 8 a.m. to 10 p.m. What is Love Anchor? **This is Canggu's open-air market** where you can find clothes, accessories, home decor, jewelry (from bracelets to necklaces to rings) that are all handmade. If you want to bring back handmade souvenirs, this is the ideal place. **Little advice**: don't hesitate to negotiate, the prices are a little high.

📍 LA BRISA

Open every day from 10 a.m. to 11 p.m. This beach club has an atypical decoration, since it is built from recycled materials and wood from old fishing boats. There you can eat, drink, chill and swim, while admiring the view of the ocean. **Honestly the view is crazy!** In addition, on Sundays from 10 a.m. it turns into a market and the atmosphere is very nice Prices from 100,000Rp.

LIVELY NIGHTLIFE

FINN'S BEACH CLUB

Open every day from 10 a.m. to 12 a.m. It is an **emblematic place** in Canggu: the Beach Club with its infinity pools, submerged bars and sunsets. You can eat there, party or simply spend an afternoon. Free entry, but drinks from Rp 40,000.

GO OUT TO OLD MAN'S

Open every day from 8 a.m. to 1 a.m. Old man's is a bar that is quite well known among tourists, it is often considered a great place for lively evenings with live music. There are often happy hours and games, including beer pong. Price from 50,000Rp per beer

GO PARTY TO MISS FISH

Open Tuesday to Sunday from 10 a.m. to 3 a.m. Miss Fish is the select red carpet private club, and evening attire required. As soon as you arrive at Miss Fish, you will be greeted by chic and sophisticated decor. The venue is designed to offer an immersive experience with its soft lighting, contemporary artwork and sofas. The DJs play right in front of you. There is also a sushi restaurant. Music style: techno, house Price from Rp 250,000

AFTER AN EVENING, TAKE CARE OF YOURSELF!

GET A MASSAGE AT THERAPY CANGGU

Open daily from 9am to 10pm Relax with a traditional Balinese massage or other wellness treatments at Therapy Canggu. It is a spa renowned for its quality services, which stands out from traditional Balinese spas. Price from 200,000Rp for a 30 min massage

TRY YOGA AT THE PRACTICE

Open daily from 7am to 6pm The Practice is one of the most renowned yoga studios in Canggu. It offers a variety of classes based on Hatha and Vinyasa yoga, suitable for all levels. The studio is a stunning space with wooden floors. Price from 140,000Rp for 90min

Luna Ola

HOUSING IDEAS

HEALTH OFFICER

Nestled in the heart of Canggu, the Luna Ola Hotel stands out because it is super modern. In fact, it was opened less than a year ago. The architecture is very elaborate and very modern. The rooms are very beautiful and the service is truly impeccable. **Anecdote:** you are 5 minutes walk from Fins beach club and the beach. Price from 62£ per night

THE SLOW

The Slow is an iconic boutique hotel in Canggu, known for its artistic design and bohemian-chic vibe. The suites are decorated with works of art. The hotel has an award-winning restaurant and an art gallery. Prices from 125£/night.

SARI AGUNG GUEST HOUSE

The place is peaceful and calm! The rooms are clean and simple. And it only takes 7-10 minutes to go to all strategic places in Canggu. It's very useful !
The price is 16£ per night

UNITED COLORS OF BALI

I spent a week in this hotel, the staff is so kind and smiling. A little thought of Eva. The villa was great! The gardens surrounding it are very beautiful; it doesn't feel like you're in the city. There is a restaurant called O'Zaromes, very good. Price from 41£ per night

TIRTHA CANGGU SUITES

I spent a weekend there. The welcome is good, the simple room, but clean and spacious, overlooks the swimming pool. It is very quiet, located in a cul-de-sac in the heart of Canggu, just two kilometers from the beach. Price from 14£/night

BARS AND RESTAURANTS

MR SPOON

Open every day from 7 a.m. to 10 p.m. **This is Bali's pastry shop,** it is well known to all influencers, there is a quiet garden and the menu is quite varied. Prices from 20,000Rp per croissant.

MASON

Open every day from 12 p.m. to midnight. It's a chic place and the food is excellent! The service is impeccable and fast, the food is very international. **Tip**: I've been there several times and recommend the chicken. It's delicious ! Price from 200,000Rp

COPENHAGEN

Open every day from 6 a.m. to 6 p.m. This café-restaurant is well known for its brunch. It is the den of nomadic foxgloves: they serve a "multiple choice" breakfast with at least three or five different options. The coffee is really good. The place is small, pretty and located on a quiet street. Prices from 60,000Rp for cocktails

GOUTHÉ STALL

Open daily from 7:30 a.m. to 11 p.m. Quaint café with a relaxed atmosphere offering French cuisine, pastries and desserts. The owners are a couple, including Jean, who is French and I must say this warung is a success! Mushroom omelette at 95,000Rp.

PENNY LANE

Open every day from 8 a.m. to 10 p.m. Very nice place, well decorated and good atmosphere! The place is rather expensive, but it is one of the very **Instagrammable** places in Canggu. The decoration is beautiful even in the toilets! Price from 100,000Rp

WAROENG BERNADETTE

Open every day from 11:30 a.m. to 10 p.m. This small restaurant has around 10 tables. Booking is recommended. The map is simple; it offers local dishes. **Be careful of the spices!** Happy hour with low prices, gin and tonic at Rp 58,000! Price from 60,000Rp

SEMINYAK : SHOPPING PARADISE

DISTANCE FROM SEMINYAK :
- Seminyak- Ubud: 1h10 depending on traffic, distance 30 km
- Seminyak- Canggu: 30 minutes after traffic, distance 9.6 Km
- Seminyak- Uluwatu: 1h after traffic, distance 26 Km

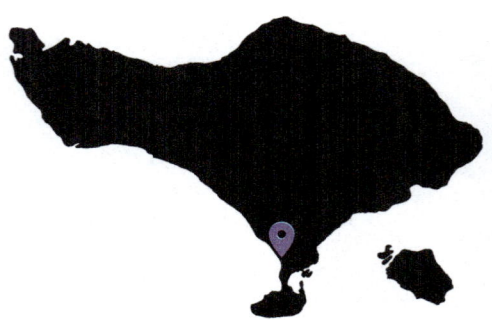

WHY VISIT SEMINYAK ?

South Bali is the most touristy area of the island. We have the advantage of being close to one of the mythical temples of Bali, the Pura Tanah Lot. Often people have difficulty distinguishing between Seminyak and Canggu, even though they are very different. Seminyak consists of more shops and hotels and is more touristy than Canggu, which is more of an expat village. Seminyak is more expensive than Kuta but more beautiful. The city is famous for its beaches and especially its shops, cafes and restaurants. We come here to party, surf and shop, there is something for everyone. There are local designers to big brands.

HERE ARE SOME TIPS AND INFORMATION :

Traffic :
- Seminyak, like Canggu, is the tourist center of the island. The traffic is crowded there; so be very careful when renting a scooter, because there are a lot of accidents. **Anecdote:** my parents spent 2 hours in traffic the week of Christmas in Seminyiak, because the traffic was saturated.

Taxis: For longer trips or in the evening, use taxis or ride-hailing services like GoJek or Grab. **Tip:** if you go out of the club, take a gojek! Don't take any risks and you'll find one at any time!

Security :
- Keep an eye on your personal belongings, especially in clubs and on the beach and when riding a scooter, especially in busy areas. In particular, at intersections on scooters, because everyone is stopping.

Recommended activities:
- Beaches: Enjoy Seminyak's beaches, known for their spectacular sunsets and surfing.
- Shopping: Browse high-end fashion boutiques, art galleries, and artisan markets for souvenirs.
- Nightlife: Explore the cocktail bars, beach clubs and nightclubs which are plentiful.

THE UNAVOIDABLE

MOTEL MEXICOLA

Open every day from 11 a.m. to 1:30 a.m. Evenings at Motel Mexicola are very well known. Firstly, the decor is very colorful and has Mexican touches. Secondly, the food is great, they are made up of Mexican specialties and also do lots of cocktails, if you are in Seminyak and looking to go out with your friends this is for you. **Tip:** the portions are very small.
Music: commercial, house.
Price from 100,000 Rp.

POTATO HEAD BEACH CLUB

Open every day from 9 a.m. to 12 a.m. This is Seminyak's beach club. It is made up of **three restaurants** and has a large swimming pool with a view of the beach. The evenings are quite nice there; the decor is very well done all along the route to access the beach club club.
Price from 200,000Rp

GO SEE THE SUNSETS AT THE BEACH

From Seminyak to Kuta, you are on the best beaches in Bali to see the sunset. Stroll on the beaches of Legian and Kuta in the south; It's really worth the detour ! There are many shops along the boulevard. You will be able to see the enthusiasm around the Kuta beachwalk or on the beach where there are many crowds. **Attention !** Do not swim: the currents are very strong and it can be very dangerous. Stay close to the edge; it's especially made for surfers. **Plus, it's free !**

📍 LA FAVELA

Open every day from 7 p.m. to 3 a.m. La Favela is as much a restaurant as it is a nightclub. Inspired **by the neighborhoods of Rio de Janeiro,** the decor is impressive and is on several levels. The cuisine offers a fusion of international and Brazilian dishes. The atmosphere is pleasant and entry is not expensive. In addition, on certain evenings, girls are entitled to free entry. Musical genre: commercial, electro.
Price from Rp 150,000 entry with consumption.

VISIT THE BOZELO STORE

Open every day from 8 a.m. to 10 p.m. It is a pleasure for me through this guide to highlight Indonesians who are setting up their businesses, Bozelo is one of them! Bozelo is a brand created in 2020 by Bobby, a young Indonesian. Today it is unmissable in Bali. In 2020, he was selling these clothes from his bedroom and now he has a store and over 10 employees! And I think it's great! The style is sportswear, but there is something for everyone. The slogan is "all eyes on you", which means "all eyes are on you". You'll see it in many of their creations: t-shirts, sweatshirts and even pants.

REVA JEWELLERY

Open every day from 10 a.m. to 9 p.m. They have just launched a second store in 2022, Laurent is the designer of the brand and his creations are of good quality. I bought some very beautiful pieces from this jewelry store for Christmas. I can tell you that there is a good quality of finish. The store is superb and the staff very professional.

GO SHOPPING IN SEMINYAK VILLAGE

Open every day from 10 a.m. to 10 p.m. It is a modern shopping center located in the heart of Seminyak; it is reminiscent of European shopping centers. At the entrance, you will find local jewelry brands. But also international brands. The shopping center is on 3 floors and honestly you have enough to find what you are looking for.

HOUSING IDEAS

W BALI - SEMINYAK

If the budget remains relatively high compared to the average price of "luxury" hotels in Bali, the W Seminyak returns it to you by ticking all the boxes of a quality Beach Resort, which is intelligently designed, well-designed and operated with high standards. If you're not yet convinced, the incredible sunsets will take care of it! the bar is quite well known in Bali and is one of the bars to do. Price from 352£ per night

COURTYARD BALI SEMINYAK RESORT

The staff is great, the swimming pool and the proximity to the beach are only a 5-minute walk away, but you can take a shuttle offered by the hotel. The location is central. Very varied and perfect breakfast: European, Asian, Balinese and others. And there are quite a few activities to do in the gardens. Price from 143£ per night

THE LEGIAN BALI

The Legian Bali is an emblematic 5-star hotel located by the sea, a very beautiful hotel opposite a magnificent beach. It consists of private villas or apartments in the building facing the sea. Very beautiful infinity pool, sunset bar and restaurant. Quality service worthy of this establishment.
Price from 436£ per night

FIRST HOTEL SEMINYAK

A hotel well located near the beach, shops, restaurants and entertainment.
The bar/restaurant is nice, the dishes are good and the breakfast buffet is provided. Very affordable price but it is nonetheless very clean. Price from 11£ per night

THE ALEA HOTEL SEMINYAK

Seminyak area hotel with cheapest prices, decent facilities. There is a swimming pool right in the middle of the hotel. The parking lot is quite spacious. The room is quite spacious; Price from 12£ per night

UMA SAPNA

The hotel is excellent! Great location, not far from the madness in Seminyak, nor the beaches and shops. The staff is super welcoming. The hotel is charming and the villas are spectacular with their swimming pools. The restaurant is good. The breakfasts are correct and à la carte. Then, the dinners and cocktails are also really good. Price from 153£ per night

BARS AND RESTAURANTS

THE FIREFLY

Open every day from 9 a.m. to 12 a.m. La Lucciola, often nicknamed "La Looch", is an emblematic restaurant located literally 3m from the beach and the sunsets are magnificent. Italian cuisine is in the spotlight, with delicious prepared dishes. The decor is very nice, it looks like a large cabin. Price from 200,000Rp

RED AND WHITE

Open every day from 12 to 10:30 p.m. Merah Putih is a contemporary Indonesian restaurant, it modernizes local cuisine and the concept is cool. The building itself is impressive, the decor is great and an innovative design. The menu is local, but reinvented!
Price from 200,000Rp

MADE'S WARUNG

Open every day from 10 a.m. to 11:30 p.m. A great restaurant for local food. The place is very large, so very pleasant for dining in privacy. The dishes are good and really inexpensive, there are often Balinese music and dance shows.
Price from 50,000Rp

SHELTER CAFÉ

Open every day from 7 a.m. to 5 p.m. Shelter is a very famous café in Seminyak; there is also a shop inside. **I recommend** going there for breakfast and trying the avocado toast.
Price from 70,000Rp

La lucciola

AMED : BETWEEN SEA AND MOUNTAINS

DISTANCE FROM AMED :
- Amed- Ubud: 2h30 depending on traffic, distance 80 km
- Amed- Canggu: 2h50 depencing on traffic, distance of 95 km
- Amed- Sidemen: 1h15 depending on traffic, distance of 38 km

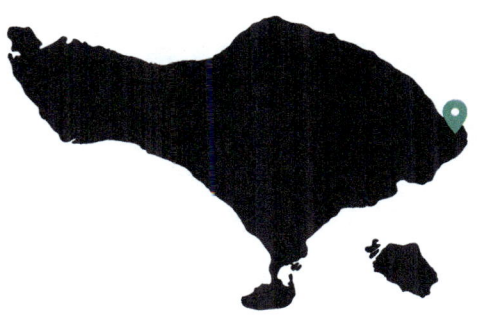

WHY VISIT AMED ?

Amed, a charming coastal village located on the east coast of Bali, is an unmissable destination, because located on the coast far from mass tourism, the atmosphere is very relaxing. Close to Mount Agung, Amed has pretty little beaches of black sand or pebbles. Don't hesitate to walk along the coast, **it's very nice.**

HERE ARE SOME TIPS AND INFORMATION :

Transport :
- Amed is accessible by car from Ngurah Rai International Airport in Denpasar, with a journey time of approximately 2.5 to 3 hours. Roads can be poor and narrow, so exercise caution.

Security :
- Amed is generally safe for tourists, but it's still a good idea to follow the usual precautions: keep your valuables safe, avoid leaving belongings unattended on the beach, and stay alert while driving.

Health and wellbeing :
- There are no major hospitals in Amed, but there are local clinics for basic health care. For more serious medical emergencies, Denpasar hospitals are best equipped. Consider taking out travel insurance including medical coverage.

Respect for local customs:
- Amed is a region where Balinese traditions are still very present. Respect local customs, especially when visiting temples.

Recommended activities:
- Diving and Snorkeling: Explore the reefs and the Liberty wreck in Tulamben.
- Hiking: Discover the surrounding hills and rice fields.
- Yoga: Take part in yoga sessions by the sea
- Boat Trips: Enjoy boat tours to watch the sunrise or sunset and go fishing.

THE UNAVOIDABLE

DIVING AND SNORKELING AT THE USS LIBERTY WRECK

Discover the wreck of the American military cargo ship USS Liberty, one of the best-known diving spots in Bali. This World War II ship is covered in coral and teeming with colorful fish. Perfect for snorkeling fans. There are plenty of diving clubs near the port that take you on the excursion costing at least Rp 500,000 per person.

BOAT TRIPS

Explore the east coast of Bali by boat; there are many fishermen who take trips along the coast. Boat trips are a good way to see what you can't see from land. Then, it's magnificent! You are alone in the world. Some stop at small wild beaches and show you lost corners: don't hesitate to go to the port to find out.

SUNSET VIEWPOINTS

Don't miss the beautiful sunsets in Amed. Lookouts like Sunset Point offer incredible vistas where you can watch the sun set behind the mountains while grabbing a drink. Bintang beer is 25,000Rp

> ### 📍 AMED BEACH
> Amed is made up of several small bays: Amed, Jemeluk, Bunutan, Lipah, Lehan and Selang. That of Lehan concentrates many jukung, but for me the most beautiful is that of Amed. This beach is lined with fishing boats that leave early in the morning. I must admit: it's part of the decor. Amed Beach is great for swimming, as the currents are not too strong and the water temperature is perfect.

A WILD COAST

SALT FARMING

Visit a salt farm and learn about the traditional method of salt production by visiting the local salt works in Amed. This is the corner of Bali that is known for this. This is a good activity to discover the local culture which allows you to learn about the ancestral techniques used by the locals to extract sea salt.

THE LAHANGAN SWEET POINT OF VIEW

Lahangan Sweet Viewpoint, near Amed in Bali, offers views of Mount Agung and the valley, rice terraces and the east coast of the island. Accessible in a 30 to 40 minute drive from Amed, this site is ideal for Instagrammers. The best time to go is early morning or late afternoon. **Little advice:** wear comfortable shoes, bring water, because there is nothing around, and respect the environment by picking up your waste.

JEMELUK BEACH

Jemeluk Beach is the perfect beach for snorkeling, as the reefs are full of corals and are very close to the shore. Then there are plenty of local restaurants along the beach which offer delicious Balinese dishes with stunning ocean views.

SWASTY DEWI SALON & SPA

Open every day from 10 a.m. to 9 p.m. A local recommended it to me, the address is known and takes locals. They even offer tea at the end of the massage. In addition, the masseuses are very professional. Price from 100,000Rp

The Lahangan sweet

HOUSING IDEAS

CORAL VIEW VILLAS

A perfect location for snorkelling. Very good restaurant on the beach. Beautiful and comfortable accommodation. The staff is very attentive. A great place to escape from the hustle and bustle of Bali, because the setting is magical, a tropical garden which gives an incredible character to this hotel.
Price from 85£ per night

MATHIS LODGE AMED

We take in the sights. The decor is splendid. Here, it's the view, the hotel is literally set in the middle of nature. Everything is decorated in harmony and is very tasteful. |There are several lodges with a magnificent infinity pool.
Price from 251£ per night

GOOD KARMA BUNGALOWS

Good Karma really caught my eye. Charming bungalows, good restaurant. Quiet, pleasant atmosphere. The only thing is that the hotel is a little far away, but the setting is magnificent. Tip: The trattoria restaurant next door is not bad.
Price from 19£ per night

BEST BEACH HOTEL

The location of the hotel is great! It is the one closest to the beaches, shops, restaurants and activities. Little extra, go to the rooftop! Price from 41£ per night

AMED BEACH VILLA

The location is the only place on the beach that is not crowded with boats. The swimming pool is very beautiful, overflowing with a direct view of the sea. The icing on the cake: right in front of the snorkling spot on the beach and adjacent to the bar which offers breathtaking views of the sunset behind Mount Agung.
Price from 71£ per night

NALINI RESORT, BALI

Small hotel by the sea with very few rooms, therefore very quiet. Ideal for those who wish to rest. The massages are very good and the food is good thanks to chef Brian who cooks very good food.
Price from 54£ per night

BARS AND RESTAURANTS

ASMAT RESTAURANT AMED

Open daily from 8am to 9:30pm Amazing place with fabulous views of the mountains and sea, very good food, their shuttle will pick you up from the seaside village and bring you here, as the road is quite steep and the Access by scooter can be very difficult. Price from 175,000Rp

WARUNG AGUNG AMED

Open every day from 11 a.m. to 9:30 p.m. Amed's friendly restaurant. A warm and smiling welcome, a great atmosphere from the owner who sings and plays at the same time, generous cuisine. If you are in Amed, **this restaurant is a must.** Price from 100,000Rp

BUKIT SEGARA RESTAURANT

Open every day from 7 a.m. to 8 p.m. The sea view from the place is just wow! The menu is very small, because it is only homemade and local dishes. It's a bit like in all restaurants. Price from 75,000Rp

OLE'S WARUNG

Open every day from 10 a.m. to 11 p.m. This restaurant is completely authentic. The menu offers typical and varied dishes at a very affordable price and of very good quality. I recommend this little address! Price from 50,000Rp

BALINESE ORIGINAL RESTAURANT

Open every day from 11 a.m. to 5:30 p.m. At the gates of Lempuyang, I invite you to take the discovery menu with 6 dishes! The welcome is friendly, a discreet place with a magical view of Mount Agung that you won't get anywhere else! Price from 200,000Rp

SANUR : LA MODERNE

DISTANCE FROM SANUR :

- Sanur- Ubud: 1h20 depending on traffic, distance of 27 km
- Sanur- Seminyak: 35 min depending on traffic, distance 14 km
- Sanur- Uluwatu: 1h20 depending on traffic, distance of 31 km

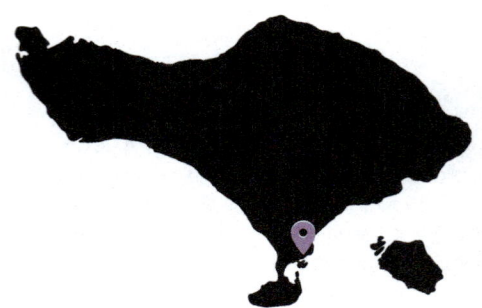

WHY VISIT SANUR ?

I chose to talk about Sanur, known for being **the first real tourist destination** on the island, especially for locals. The atmosphere is local and its beach is safe for swimming. Sanur is in full development, especially because it is the main port for traveling to Nusa Penida and Nusa Lembongan. Many developers are interested in Sanur, which is becoming a rather modern resort that attracts many Indonesians from all over the country.

HERE ARE SOME TIPS AND INFORMATION :

Transport :
- Sanur is easily accessible from Ngurah Rai International Airport, approximately 30 minutes' drive away. Here are some options:
- Taxi and Private Driver: Taxis and private drivers are available at the airport and can be booked in advance.
- Scooter Rental: Renting a scooter is a convenient option for Sanur and its surrounding areas. The roads are quiet and well maintained.
- Bike: Renting a bike is a great option to get around the Sanur promenade and explore the city at a different pace. **It's one of the only places in Bali where you can do it!**

Budget :
- Sanur is quite affordable, with plenty of dining, shopping, and accommodation options to suit all budgets.

Health and wellbeing :
- Sanur has several clinics and medical centers for basic healthcare. For more serious medical emergencies, Denpasar hospitals are well equipped.

Recommended activities
- Beach Walk: Take a stroll along the Sanur promenade, which offers a beautiful view of the ocean.
- Water sports: try kitesurfing, paddle boarding and other activities.

THE UNAVOIDABLE

ENJOY THE BEACH

The particularity of Sanur beach is that it is artificial, it looks like a lagoon. Its calm waters, protected by a coral reef, are perfect for swimming. The embankment is 4km long and you can cycle there. There are many bike rental companies. Don't hesitate to stop for a drink.

SANUR MORNING MARKET

Open every day from 9 a.m. to 9 p.m. Market to visit in the morning absolutely. All sellers offer local products. Between fruits, vegetables, meats and other dried seafood products such as small fish, etc. Visiting this place is important if you like to know more about the country and culture. It's far from classic tourist activities and it's **worth the detour!**

LE MAYEUR MUSEUM

Located near the beach, the Le Mayeur Museum was once the residence of the Belgian painter Adrien-Jean Le Mayeur de Merprès, who arrived in Bali in 1932. It houses nearly 90 of his paintings. The museum exhibits his works offering a fascinating insight into Balinese life and art.

📍 MASSIMO

Open every day from 11 a.m. to 11 p.m. It is the best Italian restaurant in Bali, it is an institution in Sanur. Known to everyone. Lots of specialties from southern Italy from which the chef comes. The terrace and interior are very nice, but it is difficult to park. Margarita pizzas at 60,000Rp.

BETWEEN BALINESE TRADITION AND MODERNITY

GO SHOPPING AT ICON MALL

Open daily from 10 a.m. to 10 p.m. Located in the heart of Sanur, Icon Mall is a must-visit destination that has just emerged from the ground. It follows the architecture of large Asian shopping centers. This modern shopping center combines Balinese charm with contemporary boutiques. Icon Mall offers a variety of international and local shops. Brands like Zara, H&M, and Uniqlo. But Sanur is known for its crafts, and Icon Mall **highlights locally made** products. Shops like Threads of Life offer traditional textiles, there **is something for everyone!**

ORCHID GARDEN AMBASSADOR VISITOR

Open daily from 8 a.m. to 6 p.m. This botanical garden features an incredible collection of orchids and other plants. It's a great place for a leisurely stroll and to take photos. It's ideal to do as a family. Entrance fee: Rp 100,000 for an adult.

SANUR NIGHT MARKET

Open every evening until 10 p.m. Spend an evening among the local stalls and take the opportunity to taste delicious specialties at unbeatable prices:
grilled fish, skewers, nasi goreng, durian... All the specialties are brought together in these places!

Icon Mall

HOUSING IDEAS

AKANA BOUTIQUE HOTEL

Located in Sanur, near the beach, it is a good restaurant where it is easy to organize excursions. The hotel has its restaurant and the cuisine is also excellent and at a very affordable price. As for the staff, always smiling, always attentive!
Price from 73£ per night

MERCURE RESORT SANUR

The particularity ? The hotel has 2 very beautiful beaches, which are wide and heavenly, with its 2 swimming pools for relaxing. You are calm. In addition, it is very well located close to shops, restaurants and bars. The staff is very welcoming, smiling, eager to make your stay pleasant. Price from 76£ per night

ARTOTEL SANUR

Close to the beach, shops, massages, restaurants and the famous Massimo, the famous ice cream parlor. The breakfast was crazy, so good that we dreamed of it at night. The staff is one of the nicest teams. In addition, they pay attention to ecology, which is rare in Asia!
Price from 108£ per night

HYATT REGENCY BALI

A very beautiful 5-star hotel decorated in local colors in the common areas.
The only drawback is the size of the hotel: with more than 300 rooms, you can get lost. However, the decor is simply impressive!
Price from 167£ per night

SUDAMALA RESORT

Place in the heart of a small, lively neighborhood and yet exemplary calm. An art gallery, a patio and a swimming pool allow you to relax. Truly a little corner of paradise. Price from 76£ per night

SANORA VILLA

Villa Sanora is another way to stay; it is possible to rent it directly. The design is very modern. In addition, it is well located in the heart of Sanur and close to shops. The staff are lovely, even by Bali standards. Price from 133£ per night

BARS AND RESTAURANTS

NAUGHTY NURI'S SANUR

Open every day from 11 a.m. to 10 p.m. The ribs were excellent and the meat tender. The service was friendly! Win, our server, was attentive and gave us good recommendations. The place is more expensive than other places, but the food is really good. Price from 110,000Rp

YOU ARE SWEET

Open every day from 6 p.m. to 10 p.m. Neat presentation, very beautiful restaurant, renowned for both the dishes and the decor. The nasi goreng is excellent. The staff is very attentive and the service impeccable. **The plus:** a grand piano and a pianist. Excellent value. Price from 200,000Rp

PIZZERIA

Open every day from 11 a.m. to 11 p.m. It was delicious. There was very tasty Fusilli pasta with Bolognese sauce. The restaurant has a nice ambiance with a live band playing quite often. The Hyatt gardens are charming. Price from 150,000Rp

LONG WARUNG

Open every day from 7 a.m. to 10:30 p.m. Close to the main street, this warung is worth the detour! Typical decor and guaranteed local restaurant. Choice of dishes not or spicy. **The black rice** was very good. This is a very good address in Sanur because it is an improved warung. Price from 80,000Rp

SIDEMEN : NATURE WAITING FOR YOU

DISTANCE FROM SIDEMEN :
- Sidemen- Ubud: 1h20 depending on traffic, distance of 33 km
- Sidemen- Canggu: 1h55 depending on traffic, distance of 51 km
- Sidemen- Uluwatu: 2h25 depending on traffic, distance of 74 km

WHY VISIT SIDEMEN ?

Sidemen, a picturesque village located in the eastern region of Bali, is an ideal destination for those looking to escape the busier touristy areas and experience a more authentic Bali. Nature is at the heart of this area, this region is made up of many rice fields and valleys.

HERE ARE SOME TIPS AND INFORMATION :

Move :
- Scooter rental: Renting a scooter is a good option for Sidemen and the surrounding area. Make sure you have an international driving license, but be careful as the roads can be poor
- Private driver: If you don't feel comfortable riding a scooter, you can rent a car with a driver for the day. Local drivers know the roads well.

Accommodation:
- Types of Accommodation: Sidemen offers varied options, from affordable guesthouses to luxury villas with views of the rice fields. Look for places with a good view. A little extra: look at the rice fields from your room.

Currency and payment:
- Cash: Small businesses and restaurants prefer cash payments, so it's good to have Indonesian rupiahs with you. There are a few ATMs in the area, but they can sometimes be out of service.

Health :
- There are a few local clinics for basic health care. For more serious medical emergencies, it is best to go to a hospital in Denpasar.
- Insect Repellent: Use insect repellent, especially if you spend time outdoors, as there are a lot of mosquitoes in this area.

THE UNAVOIDABLE

■ VISIT THE GATES IN LEMPUYANG

East Bali is home to some of the most breathtaking sights on the island, but you need to leave Ubud or Sidemen early to take photos of Lempuyang Temple's Gate of Heaven. This is one of the Instagrammable photos of Bali. The temple is very beautiful. It's worth the detour! There are many agencies or excursion booking sites that offer a package with a guided tour, a dinner and discovery of the surrounding area.

■ MOUNT AGUNG SUNRISE HIKE

An incredible hiking experience! Honestly, everyone told me that this experience is difficult, but that it was worth it, the guides are great, **the reward?** The summit has a breathtaking view.

■ DISCOVER GEMBLENG

Several things melt from it, an incredible waterfall. Firstly, an exceptional view overlooking the valley. Then there are several small pools to rest from the "climb" (5min climb on concrete markets) and to enjoy the landscape. Finally, comfort after the effort: the toilets and the restaurant at the summit. Access is sometimes difficult because the steps are narrow and there are more than one.

◉ BESAKIH TEMPLE

Open every day from 8 a.m. to 6 p.m., **the "Mother Temple" of Bali** is a vast complex of 23 temples perched at approximately 1,000 meters above sea level. The monument is very impressive and worth the detour.
The largest and most important Hindu temple in Bali. High sacred place reserved for ceremonies; come and observe the offerings. The temples cannot be visited. Entrance is 5000 Rp

IN THE HEART OF NATURE

RELAX AT KAPHA SPA

Open every day from 8 a.m. to 9 p.m. It's a perfect relaxing place, they offer a different Balinese massage, scrubs and the highlight of the show, a magnificent flower bath with an incredible view! Which makes the reputation of the place, in other words it's the dream.
Erika and Arrasih **are very talented** and very professional. I recommend ! Price from 100,000Rp

MAKE YOUR OWN JEWELRY

Open daily from 8 a.m. to 10 p.m. It happens at Silver Sidemen, where Mode will take care of you. She is a lovely person who will explain how to design jewelry and guide you through the manufacturing process.
Price from 14£ for making the jewelry

LE PONT JAUNE TUKAD YEH UNDA

Open every day
A breathtaking view! Instead, come at midday for the view. There is a restaurant right next to the bridge and the meal is excellent as is the service. And the prices are really not expensive. To do if you are in sidemen.

VISITOR TUKAD CEPUNG

Open every day from 7 a.m. to 6 p.m. Located a short hour's drive from the village of Sidemen in Bali, the Tukad Cepung waterfall is quite special. After a descent into the jungle, we arrive at a river. To the right, a small, lovely waterfall. From 10:30 a.m., there is a 1-hour queue to take a photo in the day well. Tip: arrive before 10 a.m. if you don't want to queue!
Price: 15000Rp

HOUSING IDEAS

MADE PUTU HOMESTAY

This accommodation is located with a Balinese family. Local experience guaranteed! The owners are super smiley and full of kindness. The two bedrooms with terrace and bathroom are brand new, very spacious and comfortable. Possibility of eating a good, very affordable meal on site, the accommodation is located just a 5-minute walk away.
Price from 16£ per night

BOTH VILLA GUESTHOUSE

Little corner of paradise with a view of the rice fields, regarding the rooms, they are impeccable and a little extra, a balcony with a magnificent view of the mountain and the rice fields.
But if you go to this area, it really is an ideal haven of peace for a break from a stay that can be a little hectic.
Price from 58£ per night

BIRD HILLS BAMBOO HOUSE

Many friends told me: "The best of my stay". I didn't go there personally. But the views are breathtaking and I couldn't not recommend it. It seems that the sunrise is great. It is ideal for couples because you are cut off from the world, as the rooms are located high up.
Price from 139£ per night

KUBU TARO

When we arrive there, we are surprised, because this accommodation is actually very small! There are only 2 bungalows, but that fits perfectly. The accommodation is located next to the main road, so very good in terms of access which is often a problem in more remote areas. The staff is helpful and very friendly, the food is very good, and there is a beautiful rice field and view. I recommend it 100%.
Price from 18£ per night

SAHIAN VILLA FORT

Amazing location, just outside the village, there are only fields around, beautiful scenery, no big stores. So very quiet right in the rice fields. You are in the heart of nature. You can rent a scooter directly on site, then the village is 15 minutes away.
Price from 33£ per night

BARS AND RESTAURANTS

WARUNG TIRTA UNDA

Open every day from 12 p.m. to 9 p.m. Warung full of charm overlooking the rice fields. This adorable couple offers excellent Indonesian dishes. Try the mie goreng, you won't regret it!
Price from 30,000Rp

SLEEPING GAJAH KITCHEN & LOUNGE

Open every day from 7 a.m. to 10 p.m. Upscale restaurant. The dishes are quality, Indonesian and Balinese specialties are numerous. The setting makes the restaurant's reputation.
Price from 100,000Rp

IDA'S WARUNG

Open every day from 10 a.m. to 10 p.m. Ida, the owner of this warung, is extraordinary and she always has a smile. The flavor of the dishes is very good. A special mention for the chicken curry and the vegetarian soup.
Price from 40,000Rp

WARUNG CEPIK SIDEMEN

Open every day from 12 p.m. to 12 a.m. Small typical Sidemen addresses, very good dishes, a superb view of the very nice rice fields. The satay sauce is to die for!
Price from 50,000Rp

NANA'S POOL & BAR SIDEMEN

Open daily from 10am to 9pm. An amazing place to have a meal when you visit Sidemen Village. The meal is delicious, the staff is very friendly and there are 5 rooms to stay in as well.
Price from 40,000Rp

NUSA PENIDA THE MAGNIFICENT!

DISTANCE TO NUSA PENIDA :
- Departure from the port of Sanur: 45 min by fast boat
- Canggu- Sanur: 40 min depending on traffic, distance 20 km

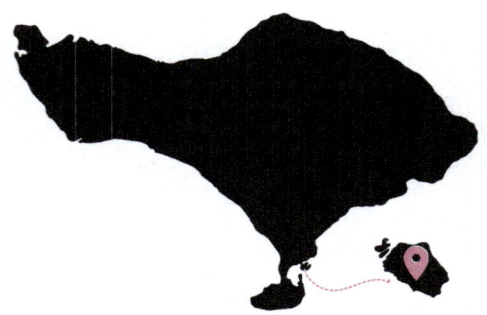

WHY VISIT NUSA PENIDA ?

Visiting Nusa Penida allows you to discover well-known landscapes with **heavenly beaches** like Kelingking and Diamond Beach. The island is known by influencers, because its Instagrammable landscapes are breathtaking! The island offers atypical activities such as diving with manta rays and exploring the beaches. In my opinion, it is an essential stopover during your stay. I myself had doubts before doing it and I must say that **I do not regret it!**

HERE ARE SOME TIPS AND INFORMATION :

How to get there: by boat:
- Boat companies: Among the most popular, Maruti Express, Scoot Fast Cruises, and Rocky Fast Cruises. It is advisable to book tickets in advance, especially in high season.

Best time to visit:
- Dry season (April to October): **ideal** for outdoor activities and diving. The weather is sunny with little rain. Plus, the beaches are more beautiful.
- Rainy season (November to March): Showers can be frequent, but the landscapes are greener. Some roads may become difficult to navigate due to mud.

Transportation on the island:
- Scooter rental: The most practical and inexpensive way. Be careful as the roads can be rough and steep with lots of turns and rocks at times.
- Car with driver: A more comfortable option, especially for families or groups. Local drivers know the roads and tourist sites well.

Safety tips :
- Roads: Be careful while driving, especially on steep and uneven roads. Always wear a helmet while scootering.
- Diving and Snorkeling: Be careful of strong currents, as manta rays are found further offshore, diving with experienced local operators is recommended.

THE UNAVOIDABLE

KELINGKING BEACH

This is the beach to see on your trip, I don't have the words. One of the most beautiful beaches in Indonesia. But, to get down there, you have to sweat. Caution, do not embark on the adventure without good cardio. Good shoes and a bottle of water are essential. Watch out for the current if you want to swim. Entrance fee at 10,000Rp/paid parking.

BROKEN BEACH ET ANGEL'S

Open from 6 a.m. to 8 p.m. We were lucky enough to be able to swim there and it's very nice despite the crowds. The two beaches are close, there is the same parking lot for access. **Be careful**, there are a lot of tourists in these places. Not much room to put your things while swimming. Be careful, there are a lot of rocks in the water. Attention ! The access roads are rather dangerous for scooters. Parking costs Rp 10,000.

ATUH BEACH

Very nice beach. She deserves it. You have to go down quite a bit to get there and it's not always easy. This beach is difficult to access with children, because the access is very steep. Swimming, on the other hand, was very pleasant. The water was turquoise and transparent, it was just magnificent.

📍 DIAMOND BEACH

After Kelingking beach, this is my second favorite in Nusa Penida. Very beautiful site, a descent which requires courage, the steps are very narrow and it is very steep, at the end it is almost climbing with the help of a rope and the energy for the ascent . Below, a very beautiful natural beach awaits you. Watch out for the powerful waves Entrance fee, 20,000Rp and paid parking.

Amok sunset

BETWEEN BEACHES AND SWIMMING POOLS

GO SEE THE SUNSET AT AMOK SUNSET

Open every day from 11 a.m. to 11 p.m. Hidden and **heavenly** place with an incredible view. We spent the day there to enjoy the infinity pools with incredible views: two towels are included, just consume. Very good and varied meal. Price from 100,000Rp

DIVING AT MANTA POINT

One of the best diving spots to see manta rays.
The Manta Point site, located in Nusa Penida, is one of the most popular diving sites in Bali and even Indonesia. Because this is where you can come, almost every day of the year, to dive with Manta rays. Attention ! The currents are very strong, given that the site is located in the open sea. **An anecdote:** when I got into the water, I was afraid of the fairly strong waves. Take care of yourself and don't hesitate to take a life jacket! Price from 16£ per session

CACTUS NUSA PENIDA

Open every day from 11 a.m. to 10 p.m. I recommend it 100%. It is one of the best beach clubs in all of Bali. The service is fast, the view is beautiful and, if you eat at the restaurant, you will have access to the swimming pool; we will lend you towels. There is nothing to say about the service. The staff is helpful and smiling. **Little extra:** if you go there by scooter after visiting Kelingking beach, you will follow roads which offer views and landscapes that are simply magical.
From 200,000Rp

HOUSING IDEAS

THE NATURE OF THE GARDEN

It's well hidden, a superb little hotel with well-appointed cabins. Great value for money and as a bonus the swimming pool which is superb in the middle of the cabins. For having stayed there: lovely staff and homemade breakfast. **Small +** the hotel is well located in relation to the places of visit. Price from 21£ per night

THE NUANCES OF PENIDA HOSTEL

The hostel is beautiful and clean. It is ideal for those who want to relax by the pool and spend more time in the hostel. Every evening they organize an event (some are paid, others not). But it's more of a relaxation hostel than a party hostel. Price from 18£ per night

THE MESARE RESORT

This hotel is in the heart of the island so ideal for visiting - the hotel offers scooters which is very practical. There is nothing around the hotel, which is ideal for peace and quiet. Yoga classes offered. The dishes are delicious! There is a mix of Balinese and international cuisines. Price from 58£ per night

SEA LA VIE RESORT NUSA PENIDA

Beautiful decor, well received and served quickly. The hotel has a beautiful infinity pool with views of the ocean and boats. The food is good and well presented. The staff are lovely. Access, as is often the case on Nusa Penida, is not easy, because the roads are very steep and sometimes in poor condition. Price from 97£ per night

MAHALOHA VALLEY

It is an isolated hotel and very well hidden, because Coral Bay is one of the few accessible beaches on the best part of the island, just past a really great little local village. The place is quiet, with a swimming pool and free-roaming monkeys visible in the trees. Diamond Bay is also very close. Price from 62£ per night

PRAMANA NATURA NUSA PENIDA

Wherever you are, the view is magnificent. The staff is extremely kind and helpful. The breakfast was very good, and so was the restaurant. I didn't have to wait to be served and the staff did everything to make my stay a success. Hotel on several levels, but small electric cars are there to take us down and up again. Price from 478£ per night

BARS AND RESTAURANTS

SECRET PENIDA

Open every day from 7:30 a.m. to 11 p.m. We went there for breakfast, facing the sea. **It's for me to do!** Little background music, pleasant service and very good dishes, well presented! It's really hot! Price from 150,000Rp

ACROPORA BAR & RESTAURANT

Open daily from 7am to 10pm Dinner with guaranteed stunning views, friendly service and staff, good food, you pay for the setting which is just crazy here.
Price from 200,000Rp

FOREST WARUNG

Open every day from 9 a.m. to 10 p.m. Address nestled in an isolated location. Local dishes prepared only when the customer has placed an order. The wait can be quite long, but everything is homemade and it's great. Price from 60,000Rp

THE CHILL PENIDA

Open every day from 8 a.m. to 10 p.m. Cozy place, attentive staff. Varied menu. Magnificent view directly overlooking the sea. Every Saturday, there is exceptional entertainment with a singer and a guitarist. It's quite well known. It's recommended to me many times. **And it's not expensive!** Price from 100,000Rp

LONTO WARUNG

Open every day from 11 a.m. to 10 p.m. I ate an excellent mie goreng there. The place is cute and discreet. All this for a price of 45,000 rupees per person, water is 10k and soft drinks are 15k. Price from 40,000Rp

Secret penida

NUSA LEMBOGAN : THE DiSCREET

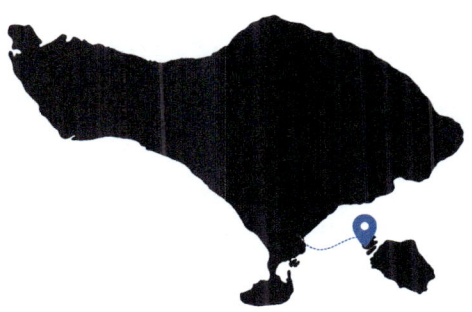

DiSTANCE TO NUSA LEMBOGAN :
- Departure from the port of Sanur: 30 min by fast boat
- Canggu- Sanur: 40 min depending on traffic, distance 20 km

WHY ViSiT NUSA LEMBOGAN ?

Nusa Lembongan is a small island off the southeast coast of Bali, known for its stunning beaches, crystal clear waters and scenery. The island is often the one most forgotten in travel guides even though for me it has as **many** interests as other places. We have the impression of being alone in the world. It is an ideal destination for those seeking tranquility and natural beauty, with plenty of activities to do on land and in the water.

HERE ARE SOME TiPS AND iNFORMATiON :

Access :
- Ferries and Speedboats: Ferries and speedboats connect Nusa Lembongan to Sanur (Bali) several times a day. The crossing takes approximately 30 minutes.
- Reservations: It is recommended to reserve your tickets in advance, especially during the peak tourist season.

Transportation on the island:
- Scooters: Scooter rental is ideal and allows you to get around easily. Be careful, there are not always helmets.
- Local Taxis: Local taxis are available for those who prefer not to drive.

Currency and Budget:
- It's convenient to have cash for small expenses, as ATMs and card payments may be limited on the island.

Health and security :
- Travel insurance: Make sure you have travel insurance that covers water activities.

Respect the environment :
- Waste: Take away your waste and use biodegradable products to protect the fragile ecosystem.
- Corals: Do not touch corals when diving or snorkeling.

THE UNAVOIDABLE

CROSS THE FAMOUS YELLOW BRIDGE

This is a must-see on the island since it is the only land crossing point between Nusa Lembongan and Nusa Ceningan. It's a bit like the San Francisco Bridge, but in miniature, because you can only cross it by scooter, the passage is narrow. To ride a scooter at least once during your stay, the landscape is very nice!

DISCOVER THE BEACHES

The southwest part of the island is home to the prettiest beaches. White sand and swimming in the quiet bay of Mushroom Beach among a few boats. Go to Sunset Beach for the sunset and to Dream Land Beach for a romantic getaway (20,000Rp). Surfing enthusiasts meet at Coconut Beach.

THE MANGROVE

Departure by canoe north of Jungutbatu for a guided tour in the mangrove. **Attention !** Don't go there alone. It is best to be accompanied by a local guide. The mangrove is made up of hidden places; with a guide, you won't miss any of the stunning scenery.

📍 THE DECK CAFÉ

Open every day from 7 a.m. to 11 p.m. The portions are generous! Good restaurant to change from Balinese restaurants! Moderate and reasonable price for the portions and good flavors! Very beautiful, with a direct view of the water and the boats! **Tip:** go there for breakfast! The dishes and the view are just wow!
Price from 70,000Rp

HIDDEN GEMS

SCUBA DIVING

Between Nusa Lembongan and the neighboring island of Nusa Penida, the seabed is full of corals. The guide told me that there were **more than 600 species of fish there.** The best known and majestic manta rays. The most famous spots are Crystal Bay and Manta's Point in Nusa Penida. **Be careful**, the dives around Nusa Lembongan are very technical, because the currents are strong. Wear a life jacket, because I assure you it can shake out a lot once you get out of the mangrove! I paid 16£ for 2 hours of diving and 3 spots.

YOGA BLISS LEMBONGAN

Open daily from 7am to 7pm. The location is superb, 5 minutes walk from the beach and all the restaurants on the main street. Very good training mixing ashtanga and yin with two very adorable, passionate and involved teachers.

KEMILAU SPA AND WELLNESS

Open every day from 9 a.m. to 10 p.m. The price is a little higher than elsewhere. But this is the best spa for me on Lembongan you can do. I recommend this place 100%. The place is magnificent, quite different from the spas you can find in Canggu.
Price from 400,000Rp

MUSHROOM BEACH

Very beautiful beach, one of the few where it is possible to swim during the day. Very good spot to enjoy the view of Bali. But on the other hand, it is one of the arrival and departure points for boats for Bali. Be careful, the entrance is quite hidden, **but there are** plenty of bars on the small beach. Don't hesitate to take a coconut: it costs Rp 20,000.

SELAMBUNG BEACH

The bay is very beautiful, it is best to walk along it, because there are a lot of boats, so it is not the ideal place for swimming. The view is breathtaking and going west the views are magnificent and on the road there will be plenty of small bars and cafes to go to, especially for the sunset.

HOUSING IDEAS

LANUSSA HILL VILLA

I enjoyed the large balcony, the hillside infinity pool overlooking the turquoise harbor and the famous yellow bridge. Really good value for money. I recommend renting a scooter, because the hotel is located in a hidden corner and access **is quite complicated.** Prices from 23£ per night with breakfast included.

THE TAMARIND RESORT

Very well located hotel, where charm and calm await you. It offers breathtaking views of Nusa Lembongan Bay, whether from the superb infinity pool or from your room, depending on its location. Price from 235£ per night

LEMBONGAN SEAVIEW

Small wooden villas facing the sea. Direct access to the sea. Very good breakfast. The hotel has an infinity pool surrounded by gardens, providing an idyllic setting in which to relax. For diving and snorkeling enthusiasts, the famous diving sites of Nusa Lembongan are easily accessible from the hotel.
Price from 42£ per night

THE ACALA SHRI SEDANA

The hotel with a splendid view of Nusa Cunigan and Nusa Penida the terrace overlooks the panorama. It is very nicely decorated. The rooms are large, the bathroom is outside. The staff is very pleasant. The breakfasts are very good and there is a choice.
Price from 63£ per night

Lanussa hill villa

Mama Mia

BARS AND RESTAURANTS

ALPONTE RESTAURANT

Open every day from 8 a.m. to 10 p.m. fabulously facing the sea, very close to the yellow bridge to go opposite. Special atmosphere at the water's edge. We tasted the pasta and desserts: everything was excellent.
Price from 60.000Rp

MAMA MiA

Open every day from 8 a.m. to 10 p.m. I had lunch one afternoon and it was very good. The restaurant's cuisine is simple, but good. The menu is varied and the view does the rest: it's magnificent! Thank you to the servers for their kindness. Price from 60,000Rp

HAi Ri ZEN

Open daily from 4 p.m. to 10 p.m. Hai Ri Zen is a restaurant located in Mushroom Bay. It offers stunning views of the bay. The restaurant specializes in Asian and Western cuisines, highlighting seafood directly caught around the island. It's ideal for a romantic dinner or an evening with friends. Price from 100,000Rp

SOKA WARUNG

Open every day from 8 a.m. to 10 p.m. Soja Warung is a truly excellent, typically Balinese warung where you can taste the specialties of the island, plus the prices are really low.
Price from 30,000Rp

JALA RESTAURANT

Open every day from 7 a.m. to 10 p.m. Pleasant restaurant with a lovely view! Very good value for money. Special mention to the yoga & surgis servers, desire, who were very attentive.
From Rp 80,000.

4. Living in Bali: Accommodation, Food and Transport

THE DiFFERENT TYPES OF ACCOMMODATiON iN BALi

Bali offers a **diverse range** of accommodation, there really is something for all tastes and budgets. In the south of the island, the offer is very developed, particularly in the hotels of Ubud, Seminyak and Nusa Dua. For greater security, **I recommend** booking on platforms like Booking or Airbnb. Plus, you will have **more choice!**

There are various options available to you:

- **Book** in a boutique hotel: these are charming establishments found in the South, more intimate, with personalized service. The emphasis is placed on a concept often around decoration, with harmony between tradition and modernity. For example: United colors of Bali

- Rent a private villa with **2 to 5 bedrooms.** Some are very luxurious with a swimming pool and sometimes a view of the rice fields. Abundant supply in the Seminyak-Canggu and Ubud region.

- Homestays are actually very popular hostels in Bali; they are very widespread on the island. **Tip:** you can stay for quite a long time in the guesthouses (several months) which can be more advantageous than I was paying 100£ per month in this rather interesting type of accommodation. It's a popular option for the quality of the welcome, the charm of the place and the cheap price. Generally, the rooms are installed in independent pavilions on one level, an ideal option for an immersive stay!

Tip: study the location carefully, because the idea is to rent a vehicle (scooter) or order a taxi to get one quickly and be closer to the tourist places.

Some **information :**

- Most hotels charge between **17 and 21% taxes.** Check that the rate includes these taxes. Breakfast is usually included.

- Reservations during high season (Dec-Jan and Jul-Aug), and in the most popular areas, at least 1 month in advance. On the gili, the prices charged can be very exaggerated in relation to the services, there is sometimes **little supply for the demand.**

- On site, especially in low season, prices are negotiated quite easily

WHERE TO EAT IN BALI: SPECIALTIES AND RESTAURANTS

Bali is a destination known for its beaches and landscapes, **but there is more to discover!** The traditional food is also very good, here is an overview of Balinese and Indonesian specialties.

Balinese culinary specialties:

- Babi Guling: Spit-roasted pork, marinated with a blend of local spices. The best is, it seems, in Kuta.
- Bebek Betutu: Stuffed and marinated duck, wrapped in banana leaves and cooked slowly, very famous in Kuta.
- Lawar: Mixture of vegetables, grated coconut, meat and spices.
- Nasi Campur: Plate of rice accompanied by various small dishes of meat, vegetables, and sambal (chili sauce).
- Sate Lilit: fish or meat skewers mixed with coconut and spices, then grilled on lemongrass stalks.

but there are also **Indonesian specialties** which are quite easily found in all restaurants, the most common are:

Nasi Goreng Nasi goreng, or fried rice, is undoubtedly Indonesia's most iconic dish. This tasty dish consists of fried rice with vegetables, eggs, and often chicken (ayam), shrimp or beef (sapi), all seasoned with a sweet soy sauce and spices. It is usually served with a fried egg and shrimp crackers (krupuk). And it's so good! Believe me, I ate them all the time.

Satay (Sate) Satays are skewers of marinated meat (chicken, beef, lamb or goat), grilled to perfection and served with peanut sauce. It's very famous **and delicious!**

Some explanations ...

- Warungs: For a traditional experience, visit the warungs, these are small family restaurants offering traditional dishes at affordable prices. It is often a couple who holds them.

- Local Markets: Markets like Pasar Sindhu in Sanur offer a variety of local foods to try.

- Cooking Class: Take a cooking class to learn how to prepare traditional Balinese dishes, often available in Seminyak or Ubud.

GETTING AROUND BALI

Despite the island's image of paradise, it is true that traffic on the island can be really complicated.

1ère option :
Taxis are widely available, especially in the south like Kuta, Seminyak and Ubud. Official taxis **like Blue Bird** are equipped with meters. Choose a taxi with a meter to avoid **scams.**

2e option :
Transportation apps like Grab and Gojek are very popular. They offer car and scooter services at affordable prices. These apps allow you to book a ride in advance. **Gede WA scooter** driver contact: +62-896-0559-7171

3e option :
Hiring a private driver can be a practical option. The private drivers know the island well and above all know how to drive Balinese style and can take you to the main tourist attractions.

4e option :
The scooter is the **most practical means** of transport. And be autonomous over small distances. The most common means of transport on the island, you will find rental companies everywhere. Request an insurance contract (it is not included in the rental price). Wearing a helmet is compulsory, certain checks take place by the police on the main roads. Contact in Canggu WA: +62-816-4743-261

Driving in Bali: things to know
- First thing, **you drive on the left** and at first it's not easy. Second, the horn is used constantly in Bali. This is not negative; it simply serves to indicate its presence. A vehicle emerging from a path has priority, so be vigilant and always keep a close eye. Watch out for animals (dogs, roosters) on the road.

- Travel times **are longer** than the distances indicated in kilometers, as there are **a lot** of traffic jams to get to the south of the island. To take into account during your journeys (average of 35 km/h).

5. PRACTICAL ADVICE AND TIPS

COMMUNICATION AND INTERNET IN BALI

During your stay in Bali, you will find that communication and internet access are relatively easy and efficient, even if you are in touristy or more remote areas including on the islands.

Bali has several mobile operators, including Telkomsel, XL Axiata, and Indosat, which provide extensive coverage on the island. **Advice:** buy a Telkomsel sim card, according to many Indonesians it is the best network and having tested it we receive reception everywhere, even on the Gili Islands! In terms of price, for 35 GB, it will cost Rp 175,000. It is true that this varies depending on the store, but it is cheaper in street stalls. **Information:** in Bali, everyone uses **WhatsApp**.

The little extra: if you stay in Bali for several months, you will only have to return there to pay for the month, without needing to change your SIM card. Tip: I know that, as a European, it is sometimes difficult to trust businesses in a foreign country. However, do not hesitate to enter a grocery store on the street: the employees are very professional and the prices are often more advantageous there. A local SIM card will not only allow you to make local calls at cheap rates, but also access the Internet.

Tip: Do not get a SIM card at the airport, as they are very expensive. While waiting for a taxi, connect to the terminal's free Wi-Fi instead. And you can buy a card directly in a supermarket or street stall; don't worry: they are everywhere!

Internet connections in Bali are generally good in tourist areas like Seminyak, Ubud, Kuta, and Canggu. Most hotels, restaurants, cafes and even beaches offer free Wi-Fi to their customers. They are absolutely everywhere, even in very remote corners. Connection speeds may vary, but are generally sufficient for browsing the web, sending emails, and using social media.

For those without a personal Internet connection, internet cafes are a convenient and cost-effective option. They are numerous in tourist areas and offer affordable hourly rates. Additionally, Bali has become a popular destination for digital nomads, and many coworking spaces have emerged, offering modern working environments with fast internet connections, meeting rooms, and cafes. Popular spaces include Dojo Bali in Canggu and Outpost in Ubud for example.

Precautions
Although Internet access is widely available, it is advisable to take some precautions to protect your personal information. Use VPN connections when connecting to public Wi-Fi networks and avoid sharing sensitive information. Additionally, some websites will be blocked and not accessible in Indonesia.

A LITTLE BAHASA

In Bali, everyone speaks English, especially in tourist places. However, sometimes some Balinese, in more remote places, have difficulty speaking English or do not speak English at all. So here's a little vocabulary. Additionally, it is always polite to say hello or thank you in the official language of the country and it will be appreciated!

TO KNOW

The Indonesian language, Bahasa Indonesia, has been the official language of the Republic of Indonesia since 1928. A particularity of Bahasa Indonesia is that it has no tense. Therefore, to know what tense is expressed in a sentence, we must look at the context, because the past and the future do not really exist. We therefore use adverbs or time indicators to mark the temporality of the sentence. For example, to use the future tense, Indonesians use the word akan. To express the past, they use telah.

A LITTLE VOCABULARY

Hello: Selamat pagi
Selamat siang (12 p.m.-3 p.m.), Selamat sore (3 p.m.-6 p.m.) Good evening (night): Selamat malam
Thank you: Terima kasih
Please: Tolong
Goodbye: Selamat tinggal
Where are you from? : Dari mana
From France : Dari Perancis
Excuse me: Permisi
Mademoiselle: nona
Monsieur: Pak / Bapak
Madame: Ibu
What is your name? : Siapa Nama Anda?
My name is Pierre: Nama saya Pierre

Yes: Ya No: Tidak
How are you? : Apa kabar?
It's going well: Kabar baik
beautiful or good: Bagus
You're welcome : Sama sama
Do you speak Indonesian? : Sudah bisa bahasa indonesia?
No, I can only a little: Tidak, bisa sedikit saja

Anecdote: bintang beer which is the Indonesian brand means star beer like Spanish estrella beer.

RESPECT FOR BALINESE CUSTOMS AND TRADITIONS

Bali is an island where customs and traditions play a central role in society. To fully enjoy your stay, it is important to respect the local culture, and for this you must understand it, it is important to familiarize yourself with certain practices and behaviors.

Religious ceremonies
Religious ceremonies are common in Bali. If you have the chance to attend a ceremony, follow these instructions:
- Stay back and do not disturb the participants.
- Do not take photos without asking permission, especially during sacred times.
- Dress appropriately and follow instructions.

The Balinese are incredibly kind and welcoming people. To show your respect and greet them:
- Greet people with a smile and a slight tilt of the head.
- Use your right hand or both hands when giving or receiving something, as the left hand is considered unclean.
- Avoid touching the heads of people, including children, as the head is considered the most sacred part of the body.

Religious offerings and symbols
You will see offerings (canang sari) everywhere in Bali, including on the sidewalks, at the entrance to guesthouses. These small offerings of flowers, rice and incense are intended for the spirits and deities; they are small colored squares that are quite easily identifiable.
- Do not step on them and avoid moving them.
- Respect the spaces where they are placed and be attentive when walking.

Photos and respect for privacy
It is true that we don't want to take photos of everything when we come, because everything is magnificent in Bali, but it is important to respect the privacy of the inhabitants.
Ask permission before taking photos of people, especially during religious ceremonies which are very symbolic for the Balinese.

Respect for natural and cultural environments
Bali is famous for its magnificent landscapes and cultural sites.
To preserve them: Do not leave waste and take your trash with you. Unfortunately, there is a lot of pollution in Bali. So, remember to take care of the island.
Avoid climbing sacred mountains without a guide, as they are of great spiritual importance to the Balinese.

AVOID COMMON TOURIST TRAPS AND SCAMS

Bali is a popular tourist destination. However, as with any tourist destination, there are certain tourist traps and scams. Here are some tips to avoid them a**nd make the most of your stay.**

- Unmetered Taxis: Choose metered taxis, like Blue Bird. If a taxi refuses to use the meter, get out and look for another one. You can also use transport apps like Grab and Gojek for transparent prices agreed on the app when ordering.

- Fake drivers: At the airport and in tourist areas, avoid unofficial drivers who approach you. Book transportation in advance or use official taxi services, the official taxis in Bali are the **"Blue Bird"**. Beware of fake taxis at the airport: they are too expensive, but also fake Grab and Gojek.

- Exchange offices: Avoid exchange offices that offer overly attractive exchange rates. Choose official exchange offices located in banks or hotels. **Always** check your money before leaving the counter. Always, when comparing several offices, the rates are displayed. The person must make the transaction in front of you and show you the exchange rate.

- Bargaining: Bargaining is common in Bali. However, be wary of sellers who excessively inflate prices for tourists. Knowing the approximate value of items can help you negotiate a fair price. Example: in Seminyak not far from the Lucciola restaurant, there are lots of small shops, don't hesitate to negotiate, because being a tourist area the prices are inflated!

- Counterfeits: Be careful of branded products offered at very low prices, as these are often counterfeits. Buy souvenirs from reputable stores to ensure authenticity. Example: in Canggu, many shoe stores sell fake pairs even though they may appear very realistic!

- Unauthorized excursions and fake guides: Book your excursions and activities with reputable travel agencies and avoid unauthorized street vendors **who may offer inferior** or even non-existent excursions. For example, at the Uluwatu temple, some people will wait for you at the checkout to show you around. This service is not official.

- Hidden prices: Make sure that the price announced for the activities includes all costs (transportation, equipment, etc.) to avoid unpleasant surprises. **Reminder:** in Bali, service taxes are added at checkout.

- Fictitious reservations: Use recognized online reservation platforms to reserve your accommodation such as Booking or Airbnb. Be wary of too-good-to-be-true deals on little-known or insecure sites.

IDEAL ITINERARY IN 2 WEEKS

I have often noticed on different Facebook groups that people who are planning a trip to Bali don't always know how to visit everything in record time, it is true that we are not in Bali **every day.** I offer you an itinerary whose duration corresponds, in my opinion, to a good balance between the pleasure of traveling and the discovery of different places. I have deliberately added points for and against so that each person can personalize their trip as best as possible. This route can also be done in another way depending on your logistical constraints. I tried to summarize as best as possible a stay over 2 weeks.

I divided this itinerary into 6 stages over 2 weeks:

- Ubud (3-4 days)
- Nusa Penida (2 jours)
- Seminyak (2 days)
- Canggu (2 jours)
- Gili Islands (2 days)
- Uluwatu (3 days)

Analysis of this route

Step n°1 Ubud:

Ideal duration: 3-4 days Distance from Denpasar airport: Approximately 1.5 hours by car

For :
- Culture and Art: Cultural centers, museums, art galleries, traditional dance shows.
- Nature: Proximity to rice terraces (Tegallalang), forests, and waterfalls (Tegenungan).
- Well-being: Renowned spas and yoga centers.

Against :
- Mass tourism: Can be very busy, especially in central areas.
- Traffic: Congested roads.

Activities and places to visit:
- Monkey Forest
- Tegallalang Rice Terraces
- Goa Gajah (Elephant Cave)
- Ubud Palace
- Blanco Renaissance Museum
- Campuhan Ridge Walk

Stage n°2 Nusa Penida :
- Ideal Duration: 2 days
- Distance from Denpasar Airport: Approximately 1 hour by car to the port + 45 minutes by boat

For :
- Landscapes to absolutely see: Kelingking Beach, Angel's Billabong.
- Snorkeling and Diving: Sites to see manta rays.

Against :
- Access: Boat crossing required.
- Infrastructure: Less developed, difficult roads.

Activities and Places to Visit:
- Kelingking Beach
- Broken Beach
- Angel's Billabong
- Crystal Bay
- Atuh Beach

Step n°3 Seminyak:
- Ideal Duration: 2 days
- Distance from Denpasar Airport: Approximately 30 mins by car

For :
- Shopping and Gastronomy: Luxury boutiques, restaurants, cafes.
- Nightlife: Beach clubs like Potato Head and Ku De Ta.

Against :
- Mass Tourism: Very busy.
- Price: Expensive compared to other more remote areas

Activities and Places to Visit:
- Seminyak Beach
- Petitenget Temple
- Eat Street (Jl. Kayu Aya)
- Double Six Beach
- Seminyak Village Shopping Mall

Stage n°4 Canggu:
- Ideal Duration: 2 days
- Distance from Denpasar Airport: Approximately 1 hour by car

For :
- Relaxed atmosphere: Surfing, yoga, cafes.
- Expat Community: Many expatriates and digital nomads.

Against :
- Rapid Development: Areas under construction, potentially noisy.
- Traffic: Roads very often congested.

Activities and places to visit:
- Echo Beach
- Batu Bolong Beach
- Tanah Lot (close to Canggu)
- Finn's Beach Club
- The Practice Yoga Stu

Step n°5 Gili Islands:
- Ideal Duration: 2 days
- Distance from Denpasar Airport: Approximately 2 hours by car to the port + 2 hours by boat

For :
- Diving and snorkeling: See turtles and colorful reefs.
- Relaxed atmosphere: No motorized vehicles, tranquility.

Against :
- Access: Boat crossing required.
- Infrastructure: Limited compared to Bali.

Activities and places to visit:
- Gili Trawangan: Lively nightlife, diving.
- Gili Air: Quiet atmosphere, snorkeling.
- Gili Meno: Peaceful atmosphere, ideal for families.

Stage n°6 Uluwatu:
- Ideal duration: 3 days
- Distance from Denpasar Airport: Approximately 1 hour by car

For :
- Beaches and Surf: Renowned surf spots (Padang Padang, Bingin).
- Culture: Uluwatu Temple with Kecak dance performances at sunset.
- Spectacular Views: Cliffs overlooking the Indian Ocean.

Against :
- Access: Steep roads.
- Price: More expensive than other regions.

Activities and places to visit:
- Uluwatu Temple
- Single Fin Beach Club
- Padang Padang Beach
- Suluban Beach (Blue Point)
- Garuda Wisnu Kencana Cultural Park

I have of course added other stops so that you can personalize your stay according to what you want.

There are several suggestions here for your stay:

1. Add Munduk

For :
- Nature and serenity: Waterfalls, rice fields, coffee plantations.
- Climate: Cooler at altitude, pleasant to escape the heat.

Against :
- Access: Winding roads, far from major cities.

Activities and places to visit:
- Munduk Waterfall
- Banyumala Twin Waterfalls
- Lac Tamblingan et Lac Buyan
- Coffee Plantations

2. Replace Seminyak with Sanur

For :
- Quiet beaches: less crowded, suitable for families.
- Water activities: Kayak, paddle, diving.

Against :
- Nightlife: Less lively than Seminyak.

Activities and places to visit:
- Sanur Beach
- The Mayeur Museum
- Bali Seawalker Tour
- Sindhu Night Market

Another optimized route
Ubud (3-4 days): Culture, nature, well-being.
Munduk (2 days): Serenity, waterfalls, coffee plantations.
Nusa Penida (2 days): Landscapes, diving.
Sanur (2 days): Calm beaches, water activities.
Uluwatu (3 days): Beaches, surfing, temples.
Gili Islands (2 days): Snorkeling, relaxation.

Conclusion :
This route offers a nice variety of experiences, I have deliberately put all the options and pros and cons so that your route is the right route. Ranging from culture to adventure and relaxation. It is of course suitable for families thanks to a good balance between activities and rest, while remaining open to other types of travelers.

100 PLACES AND ADDRESSES

UBUD

RESTAURANTS
- Pistachio
- Locavore
- Mosaic
- Locale Rain
- Bridges Bali
- Naughty Duck
- White Pair Mandif
- Sage
- Organic Cider
- Alchemy

CASCADES
- Cascade Tegenungan
- Tukad Cepung Cascade
- Cascade Kanto Lampo
- Cascade Goa Rang Reng
- Taman Sari Cascade
- Tibumana Falls
- Cascade Collect
- Cascade Letter

ACTIVITIES
- Visit to the Ubud Monkey Forest
- Exploring the Royal Palace of Ubud
- Discovery of the traditional art market of Ubud
- Walk in the rice fields of Tegalalang
- Goa Gajah Temple Visit
- Explore the Agung Rai Art Museum (ARMA)
- Participation in a Balinese cooking class
- Hike the Campuhan Ridge Walk
- Visit the temple of Taman Saraswati Temple
- Discovery of the Neka Art museum
- Excursion to the Tegenungan waterfall
- Attending a yoga session at a local studio
- Exploring the Blanco Renaissance Museum
- Coffee tasting at a local plantation
- Walk in Penglipuran village
- Discovery of the Jatiluwih rice fields
- Bali Bird Park Visit
- Participation in a traditional Balinese ceremony
- Exploration of the Komaneka art gallery

CANGGU

RESTAURANTS

- The Shady Shack
- Betelnut Cafe
- Crate Cafe
- Bu Mi's Warung
- Milk & Honey
- Peloton Supershop
- Moana Fish Eatery
- Deus Ex Machina
- The Loft
- Fishbone Local
- Mason
- Bali Bowls & Smoothies
- Sea coffee
- Ettore Gelato
- Touch
- Double
- Treasure garage
- Sushi
- Milu By Nook et Passo by Nook-Cemagi

EVENING

- Luigi's (pizza bar/restaurant) free before 10:30 p.m. otherwise 100,000Rp
- Sand Bar, DJ evening on the beach every evening from 11 p.m.-midnight // before 9 p.m. Live concert)
- Free Vault

ACTIVITIES

- Surf
- Batu Bolong Beach
- Echo Beach
- Plage de Berawa
- Tanah Lot Temple
- Canggu Beach
- Pererenan Beach
- Spa and wellness
- Canggu Market
- Old Man's Bar
- Finn's Beach Club
- La Brisa Beach Club

SEMINYAK

RESTAURANT
- Bamboo
- Sisterfields
- Métis
- Last
- Ginger Moon
- Revolver Espresso
- Sea Circus
- Sardine
- Mamasan
- Boy'N'Cow
- Mrs Sippy
- Bikini Restaurant

EVENING
- Shishi (club comprising two rooms, one electro and one commercial) free for girls; 250,000 Rp for the boys with a drink. On Wednesdays, it's free for girls and drinks last until 11 p.m.
- The favéla (commercial) free for girls and 150,000Rp for boys
- Da Maria (nice – electro and commercial evenings)

ACTIVITIES
- Shopping à Seminyak village, Seminyak square,
- Relaxing on Seminyak Beach
- Visit to spas and wellness centers
- Surf lessons
- Cocktails at beach bars and clubs
- Visit temples including Pura Petitenget
- Stroll through art galleries and workshops

STORE
- Normal
- Magali Pascal
- Drifter Surf Shop
- Paul Ropp
- Lily Jean
- Bamboo Blonde
- Uma and Leopold
- The Flea Market Seminyak
- Mister Blonde
- Body & Soul
- Report

KUTA

RESTAURANT
- Hotel Indigo (restau + pool)
- Zanzibar
- The sand
- Poppies Restaurant
- Made's Warung
- Fat Chow
- Hard Rock Cafe Bali
- Jamie's Italian Bali
- Indonesian Warung
- Rosso Vivo Dine & Lounge
- Kori Restaurant & Bar
- Bamboo Corner
- Spice Mantra

STORES
- Beachwalk Shopping Center
- Discovery Shopping Mall
- Lippo Mall Kuta
- Kuta Art Market
- Bali Mall Galleria
- Kuta Square
- Matahari Kuta Square
- Bali Brasco
- Park 23 Mall
- Carrefour Transmart
- Kuta Leather and Tailor
- Sogo Department Store

ACTIVITIES
- Surf
- Shopping à Beachwalk, Mali gallery,
- Visite du Waterbom Bali
- Massages and spas
- Visit local temples
- Jet ski
- Amusement parks for children
- Relaxation on the beaches
- Visit to local markets
- Nightlife in bars and clubs
- Exploring traditional villages

SIDEMEN

RESTAURANT
- Warung Maha Neka
- The Bukit Artha
- Cardamom Kitchen Stall
- Ida's Warung
- Warung Cepik
- Check out Sawah Restaurant
- Samanvaya Rice Terrace Restaurant
- Joglo D'Uma
- Warung Ume New
- Radha Warung
- Sawah Indah Resto
- Warung Melita
- Wapa's Restaurant
- Subak Tabola Villa Restaurant
- The Siddhartha
- Enak's Warung
- Warung Deva
- Mangosteen Garden
- Warung Agung
- Bukit Luah

ACTIVITIES
- Hiking in the rice fields
- Visit of Tukad Cepung Waterfall
- Visit the Gembleng Waterfall
- Visit to Yeh Labuh Waterfall
- Yoga and meditation
- Spa and massages
- Rafting on the Telaga Waja River
- Visit to coffee and spice plantations
- Tea and coffee tasting
- Exploring local temples
- Horse riding

CASCADES
- Tukad Cepung Cascade
- Cascade Whole
- Cascade Yeh Poh
- Jagasatru Cascade
- Cascade Yeh Long

LOVINA

RESTAURANT

- Apple Store
- Jasmine Kitchen
- Dolphin Shop
- Warung Ayu
- Lovina Seafood Barbeque
- Bamboo Stall
- Jegeg's Warung
- Kakatua Warung
- Warung Yess
- Warung Tirta Sari
- Warung Made
- Kadek Coffee Shop
- Ari's Warung
- Caucasian Warung
- Goddess's Warung
- Warung Damar
- Mina's Warung
- Mak Beng's shop
- Taste Stall
- Warung Sri

ACTIVITIES

- Dolphin watching
- Scuba diving
- Snorkeling
- Bathing in Banjar Hot Springs
- Visit the Brahma Vihara Arama Buddhist Monastery
- Hike to Gitgit Waterfalls
- Boat ride
- Exploring the Singaraja Market
- Visit to Beji Temple
- Visit of the Gedong Kirtya museum

BEACHES

- Lovina Beach
- Pemaron Beach
- Antura Beach
- Tukad Mungga Beach
- Kaliasem Beach

SANUR

RESTAURANT

- Maximum
- Three Monkeys Sanur
- Little Bird Stall
- Soul in a Bowl
- Lilla Beach
- Art Cafe Sanur
- Gong Restaurant
- The Porch Cafe
- Mak Beng's shop
- Batu Jimbar Cafe
- The Fire Station
- Dining room
- Cinnamon
- Casablanca Dine Drink Dance
- Char Ming
- Mona Lisa Cafe
- Arena Pub & Restaurant
- Pregina Warung
- Mezzanine Bar & Restaurant
- Retro Cafe

ACTIVITIES

- Shopping at Icon mall
- Traditional fishing
- Boat trips
- Visit local temples
- Sunbathing on black sand beaches
- Exploring traditional villages
- Visit to local markets

BEACHES

- Sanur Beach
- Sindhu Beach
- Karang Beach
- Mertasari Beach
- Semawang Beach
- Sunrise Beach
- Segara Ayu Beach

AMED

RESTAURANT

- Sails Restaurant
- Galaga
- Delicious Warung
- The Grill Bar & Restaurant
- Taste Rest
- Blue Earth Village
- Waroeng Santa "Fe"
- Ole's Warung
- Komang John's Cafe
- Hita Bebek Park
- Beach Stall
- Apneas
- Amed Cafe
- Good Karma Restaurant
- Same Same Cafe
- Delicious Beach Restaurant
- Pacha Bar and Restaurant
- Meeting Point

ACTIVITIES

- Scuba diving
- Snorkeling
- Hike Mount Agung
- Visit to shipwrecks
- Traditional fishing
- Yoga and meditation
- Boat trips
- Exploring the rice terraces
- Visit local temples
- Sunbathing on black sand beaches
- Dolphin watching
- Exploring traditional villages
- Visit to local markets

BEACHES

- Amed Beach
- Jemeluk Beach
- Lipah Beach
- Selang Beach
- Bunutan Beach
- Lean Beach

ULUWATU

RESTAURANT
- Karma beach
- El Cabron
- The Edge Bali
- Everything Dayclub
- Sundays Beach Club
- The Shack
- The Loft
- Drifter Cafe and Restaurant
- Where is Uluwatu?
- Vessel Stall
- Bukit Cafe

EVENING
- Catwee Tree: Free entry. Beer at Rp 30,000. Renowned for being the Thursday evening in Uluwatu. Tip: arrive around 9 30 p.m. This is also a good "before" time.
- Hatch: Free entry (except for certain events). Beer at Rp 30,000. Come there for 11:30 p.m. It's perfect for an "after" party. The DJs are good and there's even a tattoo parlor in the club.
- Rolling Fork: free entry, beer at Rp 20,000 and Latin evenings every Tuesday. It's just great! The atmosphere is crazy!

BEACH
- Karma beach
- Padang Padang Beach
- Suluban Beach (Blue Point Beach)
- Bingin Beach
- Dreamland Beach
- Thomas Beach
- Nyang Nyang Beach
- Balangan Beach
- Karma Beach
- Pandawa Beach
- Impossible Beach
- Nusa Dua Beach

ACTIVITIES
- GWK Cultural Park (show and one of the largest statues in the world)
- Visit Uluwatu Temple
- Attend a Kecak dance performance
- Surf the famous surf spots
- Spend a day at the beach clubs

NUSA PENIDA

RESTAURANT
- Virgin beach
- Warung Tu Pande
- Penida Colada
- The Gallery Nusa Penida
- Cottage Stall
- Secret Penida Restaurant
- Amok Sunset
- Ogix Warung
- Jungle Warung
- Coco Penida Restaurant
- Sunny Cafe Penida
- Penida Espresso
- The Krusty Krab Penida
- Organica Fresh and Tasty Food
- Jukung Warung

BEACH
- Kelingking Beach
- Diamond Beach
- Atuh Beach
- Crystal Bay
- Broken Beach
- Angel's Billabong
- Suwehan Beach
- Tembeling Beach and Forest
- Peguyangan Waterfall and Beach
- Banah Cliff Point Beach

DIVING
- Nomads diving: diving or snorkelling (between 400 k and 1.5 m) swimming with manta rays in both cases, we saw turtles, two diving spots (9 a.m. - 3 p.m.) Contact: +62 813 39079985

ACTIVITIES
- Nusa penida tour travel (+62 812-4621-9466) 41£ per person can be ready, for 2 days, boat, hotel (1 night) driver both days on the island and the lunch restaurants) very profitable! Possibility of taking the return boat a few days later.

NUSA LEMBONGAN

RESTAURANT
- The Deck Café & Bar
- Sandy Bay Beach Club
- Indiana Kenanga Restaurant
- Lemongrass Bar & Restaurant
- Lembongan Beach Club & Resort Restaurant
- Bali Eco Deli
- Muntigs Bar & Restaurant
- Thai Pantry
- Ohana's
- Tigerlillys Restaurant

ACTIVITIES
- Snorkeling
- Exploration of the mangrove
- Visit from Devil's Tear
- Walk on the yellow bridge
- Discovery of Dream Beach
- Sandy Bay Tour
- Kayak
- Stand-up paddle
- Visit to the Devil's Cave
- Exploration of Jungut Batu beach
- Visit the Segara Temple temple
- Visite de Gala-Gala Underground House
- Exploring Tamarind Beach
- Panorama Point Tour
- Excursion to Nusa Ceningan
- Snorkling guide (turtle, rays, mangroves for 250k) +62 821-4451-7793

BEACHES
- Jungut Batu Beach
- Mushroom Bay Beach
- Dream Beach
- Sandy Bay Beach
- Tamarind Beach
- Mangrove Beach
- Song Lambung Beach
- Secret Beach
- Sunset Beach
- Coconut Beach

GILI TRAWANGAN

RESTAURANT

- Scallywags Seafood Bar & Grill
- Pituq Waroeng
- The Banyan Tree
- Pearl Beach Lounge
- Jali Kitchen
- Kayu Cafe
- Pituq Cafe
- Same Same Reggae Bar
- Egoiste Beach Restaurant & BBQ
- Little Gili

ACTIVITIES

- Scuba diving
- Snorkeling
- Turtle watching
- Sunset cruises
- Kayak
- Stand-up paddle
- Visit to the night market
- Outdoor cinema
- Bike ride around the island
- Relaxation on the beaches
- Nightlife and beach bars
- Snorkling guide (turtle, rays, mangroves for 250k) +62 821-4451-7793

BEACHES

- Northeast Beach
- Southeast Beach
- South Beach
- West Beach
- Sunset Point Beach
- Turtle Point Beach
- Malibu Beach
- Plage de North Beach
- Plage de Central Beach

BOAT

- Fast boat: approximately 33£ return: +62 852 37954309 from Padangbai

Gili MENO

RESTAURANT
- Mahogany Beach Restaurant
- We'Be Café
- Sasak Café
- Little Bali Restaurant
- The name of Mojo Beach Resort Restaurant
- Karma Beach Gili Meno
- Same Same Bar & Restaurant
- Jali Cafe
- Rust Less
- Adeng-Adeng Beach Restaurant

ACTIVITIES
- Scuba diving
- Snorkeling with turtles
- Tour of the island on foot
- Glass bottom boat trip
- Yoga classes
- Kayak
- Relaxation on the beaches
- Horseback riding
- Visit to the turtle sanctuary
- Fishing excursion
- Massage and spa sessions
- Birdwatching at Gili Meno Bird Park

BEACHES
- Gili Meno Beach
- Turtle Point Beach
- Secret Beach
- Sunset Beach
- Mangrove Beach

BOAT
- Fast boat: approximately 33£ return: +62 852 37954309 from Padangbai

Gili Air

RESTAURANT

- Pachamama Organic Cafe
- Mowies on the Beach
- Scallywags Beach Club
- Chill Out Bar & Bungalows
- Ruby's Cafe
- Captain Coconuts Gili
- Italian classic
- Puri Pandan Restaurant
- The Mexican Kitchen
- Zipp Bar Restaurant
- Sharkbites
- Biba Beach Cafe
- Gili Bliss Gili Air
- Sunny's Warung
- Another Bar & Restaurant
- Raja Bar & Restaurant
- Bamboo Stall

BOAT

- Fast boat: approximately 33£return: +62 852 37954309 from Padangbai

BEACH

- Sunset Beach
- East Beach
- South Beach
- North Beach
- Gili Air Beach
- Turtle Beach
- Mowies Beach
- Scallywags Beach
- Sunrise Beach
- Gili Lumbung Beach

ACTIVITIES

- Snorkelling (with turtles and 1000 species of fish) -> Gili Meno possibility of just taking boats to go to the island (about 10 minutes by boat, take a mask and snorkel and go swimming with the turtles alone) otherwise take a boat which takes you to the turtle spot

FiNALLY ALL I HAVE LEFT TO TELL YOU iS

HAVE A GOOD TRIP !

Despite the significant work involved in writing this guide, this guide is not immune to last minute changes. Don't forget to share your comments and discoveries with us.

In accordance with consistent case law (Toulouse 14-01-1887), any involuntary errors or omissions which may have remained in this guide despite our care and editorial controls cannot engage my responsibility. All rights of translation, reproduction and adaptation reserved for all countries.

The information contained in this travel guide is provided for general information purposes only. Although we endeavor to keep this information up to date and accurate, we make no representations or warranties, express or implied, as to the completeness, accuracy, reliability, suitability or availability of this information, products , services or contacts for activities and guides mentioned in this guide.

The inclusion of any contact or service in this guide does not constitute a recommendation or endorsement by us. Users of this guide are encouraged to make their own due diligence and exercise their own judgment when engaging service providers or participating in activities.

Under no circumstances will we be liable for any damage or loss, whether direct or indirect, or any other damage or loss, howsoever arising, resulting from loss of data or profits arising out of, or in connection with with, the use of this guide.

Users of this guide should be aware that they participate in activities and engage in services at their own risk. It is strongly recommended to take out adequate travel insurance covering the planned activities.

By using this guide, you accept this disclaimer and agree that we will not be held responsible for any claims, losses or damages arising from the use of the information, contacts or services mentioned in this guide.

ISBN : 9798332744594

Printed in Great Britain
by Amazon